A Speaking Life

In Memoriam

ARTHUR MICHAEL RAMSEY

Bishop, Priest, Pastor
and
Seer of Glory

A Speaking Life

John Keble & the Anglican Tradition of Ministry & Art

Edited by Charles R. Henery

This book has been produced in conjunction with Nashotah House, Wisconsin

First Published in 1995
Gracewing
Fowler Wright Books
Southern Avenue, Leominster
Herefordshire HR6 0QF

Gracewing Books are distributed

In New Zealand by
Catholic Supplies Ltd
80 Adelaide Road
Wellington
New Zealand

In Australia by
Charles Paine Pty
8 Ferris Street
North Parramatta
NSW 2151 Australia

In Canada by
Meakin & Associates
Unit 17, 81 Auriga Drive
Nepean, Ontario, KZE
7YS
Canada

In U.S.A. by
Morehouse Publishing
P.O. Box 1321
Harrisburg
PA 17105
U.S.A.

Photographs 1, 3, 4, 5 appear by kind permission of the Henry Moore Foundation, Much Hadham, Hertfordshire.

Front cover Photograph and photograph 2 are copyright of John Donat AAdip RIBA, 38 Regents Park Road, London NW1

Cover design by Gill Onions

Typesetting by Action Typesetting Limited, Gloucester
Printed by Cromwell Press, Broughton Gifford, Melksham, Wiltshire, SN12 8PH

Contents

Contributors

CHARLES R. HENERY is Assistant Professor of Church History and Homiletics in The John Maury Allin Distinguished Professorship at Nashotah House. He acted as Convener of the North American Commemoration of the Bicentenary of the Birth of John Keble, held at Nashotah in 1992. He is editor of *Beyond The Horizon: Frontiers for Mission* (1986), and has a long-standing interest in Episcopal Church history, especially on the role of bishops in the development of religious life in America.

THOMAS P.M. DEVONSHIRE JONES is Vicar of St. Mark's Church, Regents Park, London. His special interest is in the field of visual arts and he presently is doing a study of 'The Best Art Work for Churches in the United Kingdom, 1972–1992' for the Sainsbury Family Trusts. In 1991 he organized an international seminar in London entitled 'The Arts and Christianity Inquiry' and more recently a 'Theology and Art Study Day' at the National Gallery. He is a contributor to various journals, among them the ecumenical publication *Church Building* of which he is a member of the editorial advisory committee.

DOUGLAS GEOFFREY ROWELL is Bishop of Basingstoke. He was formerly Fellow, Chaplain, and Tutor in Theology at Keble College, Oxford, and a University Lecturer. He has served on the Church of England Liturgical Commission and was a member of the Doctrine Commission. He also has acted as honorary director of the Archbishop's Examination in Theology. In 1983 he organized the Oxford Movement Sesquicentennial Conference and more recently the Keble Commemoration in Oxford University. His several published works include *The Vision Glorious: Themes and Personalities of the Catholic Revival In Anglicanism* (1983), and *The English Religious Tradition and the Genius of Anglicanism* (1992).

GORDON S. WAKEFIELD is a Methodist Minister in the United Kingdom. In 1979 he was appointed the first non-Anglican Principal of the Queen's College at Birmingham. He has written extensively in the field of spirituality, is editor of *A Dictionary of Christian Spirituality* (1983), and author of *Bunyan the Christian* (1992). He was invited to give the Bible studies for the Anglo-Catholic Congress at Loughborough in 1983. In 1986 he was awarded the Lambeth Doctorate of Divinity for his work in scholarship and ecumenism. He is a founder member and a President of the Ecumenical Society of the Blessed Virgin Mary, and President of the Methodist Sacramental Fellowship.

J. ROBERT WRIGHT is St. Mark's Church in the Bowerie Professor of Ecclesiastical History at The General Theological Seminary, New York City. He is a member of the Commission on Faith and Order of the World Council of Churches, the Standing Commission on Ecumenical Relations of the Episcopal Church and the Anglican-Roman Catholic International Commission. He recently served as President of the North American Academy of Ecumenists and is now Honorary Canon Theologian to the Bishop of New York. In 1981 he was elected a Life Fellow of the Royal Historical Society in London. His numerous publications include *Prayer Book Spirituality* (1989) and *The Anglican Tradition* (1991).

Foreword

That this volume is dedicated to the memory of Michael Ramsey will move the heart of any who knew that great Anglican personally and are aware that they owed a debt to his profound spirituality. In his time as a bishop and then archbishop he often visited the United States and formed many American friendships. But the place which he came to find as like a second home to him, and where he felt his own life of the spirit to be most fulfilled, was Nashotah House.

It is right that the House should celebrate its hundred and fiftieth anniversary with a conference on John Keble, for it is also the two hundredth anniversary of his birth; and Keble stood for the best of the Anglican pastoral and priestly ideals and personally helped to raise the standards of worshipping life and habits of prayer and pastoral care; and not only among Anglicans, for Sir John Reith, the creator of modern British broadcasting, used to tell how his strongly Presbyterian mother in Scotland made him learn Keble's poem for each Sunday on that day. There was something so quiet about Keble, so unpretentious, so high-principled and yet without aggression or fanaticism, so poetic and even lyrical at times; the sweet-natured country pastor of an old school which yet adapted to the new Victorian generation.

The book is fortunate to have Dr. Geoffrey Rowell who is the leading expert on Keble in our day and has had the privilege to be himself the priest in charge of the chapel that was built in Keble's memory; to have Professor Robert Wright who has done so much to clarify and forward the ecumenical relations of the episcopal tradition, especially by his ability to set them always in a long historical context; to have Dr. Gordon Wakefield who has shown, as no one else ever did before, the catholic inheritance within Methodism, and who has illuminated the Anglican tradition far better than some professed Anglican writers; and to have a present-day working parish priest in a city, Thomas Devonshire Jones, with his special contribution on the relation of art and architecture to religious worship.

It is clear that this book will be found of special importance at this time when churches need to seek out their roots and look especially to the quality of their inheritance in spirituality and pastoral care.

Owen Chadwick
Cambridge

Introduction

On Maundy Thursday, 29 March 1866, a country parson in England finished the course of his earthly ministry. He would have lived unknown, but at his death he was widely honoured. Praise for the glory of creation and reverence for the mystery of God were his undoing. Once he had set these lofty movements of the heart to poetical song his light could not be hidden.

The author of *The Christian Year* naturally invited attention. His poetry awakened a spiritual vision, offering a fresh awareness of God's intimate presence in daily life. For the many who found such refreshment, the mind and character of the man who was able to pen such verse was wonderfully attractive. Even more so was this true for those who responded to his genuine love for the catholic and apostolic faith. His defence of the primitive foundation of the Church of England only strengthened this bond. While his own quiet, steady pastoral labors, his self-forgetfulness in ministry but never the forgetfulness of his people, bore still eloquent and convincing testimony to the holiness of the church to which he remained so loyal.

John Keble was rightly esteemed in his day as the original source and real spirit of the Oxford Movement.[1] His life embraced the whole history of the first phase of that great church revival, and lasted long enough to enter upon the second, with its catholic worship and ritual. His life witnessed as well the budding of the Anglican Communion in the unfolding light of this revival. The saintly vicar of Hursley died a year before the first Lambeth Conference in 1867, when there assembled 'Bishops of Christ's Holy Catholic Church in visible Communion with the United Church of England and Ireland, professing the Faith delivered to us in Holy Scripture, maintained by the Primitive Church and by the Fathers of the English Reformation.'[2]

John Keble was born in 1792. As it happens, this was also the year of the first consecration of a bishop in the newly independent Episcopal Church here in America. The event was little noticed in England, with the mother church there showing little interest in her dubious offspring on the other side of the Atlantic for the next generation. Indeed, as late as 1823, one English prelate was astonished to learn that the American church had bishops of some type 'such as we are'. Communication between the two churches was such that the American presiding bishop declined in 1822 to provide a letter of introduction for a priest traveling abroad. 'I know not a Correspondent remaining in England,' William White unhappily confessed.[3]

Anglican fellowship was stimulated by the arrival in England in 1823 of two American bishops, John Henry Hobart of New York and Philander Chase of Ohio. In differing ways, these two colorful men captured the imagination of English church members. Hobart's writings were familiar to a group of High Churchmen in England, and indeed Hugh James Rose, the vicar of Hadleigh, regarded the New Yorker as the most authoritative voice of the day on apostolic order and episcopacy. To a younger set of clerics, who were destined to emerge as leaders in the catholic revival, Hobart was a striking personality, and his intriguing mixture of High Church principles and American democratic ideals made him attactive to them. He bore the countenance, said Walter Farquhar Hook, of 'one who has stood firm in the hour of peril, and who has fought, and will fight, the good fight.' Another who was drawn to this transatlantic apostle was a new fellow of Oriel College, John Henry Newman. Thirteen years after meeting Hobart, Newman fondly spoke of the American 'whose memory is interesting personally to many around us who saw him when in England,' and described him as 'so considerable a man.'[4]

No one who learned of the American church through Hobart was likely to be unimpressed. To his English listeners he made plain the primitive character of his native church and was unabashed in his zeal for her catholic life and witness. This commanding personal testimony made inevitable a reconsideration of the nature and identity of

Anglicanism. As Newman, in fact, wrote some years later:

> This is our own special rejoicing in our American rela-
> tions; we see our own faces reflected back to us in
> them, and we know that we live. We have proof
> that the Church, of which we are, is not the mere
> creation of the State, but has an independent life,
> with a kind of her own, and fruit after her own
> kind ... The American Church is our pride as well
> as our consolation.[5]

Keble does not appear to be among those who made the
acquaintance of the bishop of New York; however, Hobart's
counsel that reform of the church should proceed from the
church itself was not lost on the future Tractarian. In 1827
Keble asked his friend John Coleridge to find him a book
treating the question of church and state relations. In particular, he sought information as to what was happening in
America. This request, as a biographer observes, marked the
beginning of an abiding interest on the part of Keble both
in the issue of establishment and in the Episcopal Church
in America.[6]

In the footsteps of Hobart and Chase there followed a
steady stream of American clergy to England, strengthening
the growing ties between the two churches. Many of these
visitors were eager to meet the author of *The Christian Year*
and often, much to their delight, were graciously received
by him. Among them was Charles McIlvaine, successor to
Chase in Ohio and a fellow member of the Evangelical
school, who met Keble at Oxford in 1835. In common
with many of those who met him, the American bishop was
struck by Keble's simplicity, describing him afterwards as
very plain in appearance and very retiring, indeed 'timid
as a deer'. He was surprised also to find that Keble was
ignorant of an American edition of *The Christian Year*.[7]
This edition had been published the year before by George
Washington Doane, the High Church bishop of New Jersey,
who regarded the work as a splendid Anglican apologetic. In
1841, Doane himself had the pleasure of staying at Hursley
vicarage, recording approvingly in his diary that the little,
old stone parsonage was 'a very nestling place for a poet.'[8]

Significantly, the warm hospitality of the Keble household to Bishop Doane took place on the occasion of the overseas visitor's presence as preacher for the consecration of the new parish church in Leeds, an event that consummated the recent act by Parliament formally establishing a principle of intercommunion between the Church of England and the American church.

The bonds of catholicity between the two churches reached a high point in 1852. That year the archbishop of Canterbury invited the American episcopate to send a delegation, on the third Jubilee of the Society for the Propagation of the Gospel, 'to manifest the essential unity of the sister Churches of America and England.' The celebration witnessed for the first time representation from all churches in communion with Canterbury and firmly planted the seeds of the future Lambeth Conference. Among the American representatives was William Heathcote DeLancey, the bishop of Western New York. To him an invitation came from Keble to preach in the parish church of St. Mary's in Hursley, adding another seal to Anglican union. And still later, it was 'a peculiar gratification' to the American delegation that Keble, although a retiring country vicar, had hastened to meet them in Liverpool on their departure and was present with others for a 'parting celebration of the Supper of the Lord.'[9]

Not surprisingly, when news of the death of John Keble reached America affection for the English priest was unreserved. The occupant of Hobart's seat in New York, Horatio Potter, in a letter to the clergy and laity of his diocese, expressed the heartfelt gratitude of many for the uncommon voice of this 'most modest and most retiring of saintly men.' As one privileged to enjoy his society and conversation, Potter gave testimony to a life filled with qualities 'no less wonderful than his seraphic poetic genius.' And he appealed to all who appreciated 'the genius and saintly worth of the departed' to unite 'in some fitting Memorial that shall testify our reverence and love, and at the same time our entire sympathy with our brethren of the Anglican Church in the loss which they have sustained.'[10]

Among the proposals for a memorial was the erection of a 'Keble Hall' at Nashotah House, in the recesses of the

American West. The seminary had been founded in 1842 on the Wisconsin frontier by three young deacons who had answered the call to aid in the apostolic labors of Jackson Kemper, the first missionary bishop of the Episcopal Church. The American concept of missionary bishops had fired the imagination of several in England, especially within Tractarian circles. It was natural that similar interest would be taken in the welfare of the fledgling Nashotah mission, particularly since it aimed to establish a religious brotherhood both to evangelize the West and to educate clergy from the native soil to advance the gospel. Edward Pusey, writing to Doane in 1843, related that news of the frontier institution under Bishop Kemper 'cheered us much,' and expressed his own personal hope that 'something monastic, involving a higher, self-denying life, with fuller devotions' might begin in America.[11] To establish a memorial to Keble at Nashotah seemed then to be most fitting, and would offer, as it was hoped, 'a lasting proof of the world-wide fame of the poet, among the men of his own age.'[12]

However, a Keble Hall at Nashotah House was not to be. Now, as providence would grant, in commemoration of the sesquicentennial of the House, this volume of essays is published in tribute to John Keble and to mark the bi-centenary of his birth. These anniversary essays, originally delivered as a series of lectures at Nashotah in the autumn of 1992, and subsequently revised for publication, provide not only a portrait of an Anglican saint who continues to inspire Christians today, but also an examination of the priestly life and pastoral care, and the place of the arts in the Anglican tradition. The portrait of Keble painted by Bishop Rowell in the first three essays handsomely delineates the features of the man as priest, pastor and poet, the three epithets by which the Church of England remembers him in her calendar today. It is a vibrant portrait, made alive by the skillful way in which Keble is allowed to speak for himself. Next, adding dimension to the first term by which he is remembered, the ideals of priesthood to which the famed vicar of Hursley bore witness are shown by Dr. Wright to be deeply rooted in Anglicanism. Indeed, as his distinctive and seminal essay xvi *A Speaking Life*

argues, there is a remarkable consistency in the Anglican doctrine of the priesthood, a consistency that reaches back to the primitive age of Christianity, and which has remained unchanged in its essentials to the present day. In Anglican pastoral tradition, Keble has quite properly taken an honoured seat and this tradition is critically and appreciatively surveyed by Dr. Wakefield, who perceptively examines the peculiar questions which confront it in the present day. The last essay examines the artistic spirit in Anglicanism. Taking an area not generally associated with Keble, Tom Devonshire Jones thoughtfully sketches the place of the visual arts in the life of the church and focuses on a modern descendant of Keble who equally reverenced the mystery of divine grace and understood the need for the services of both theology and art in this adoration. For those present at the Nashotah commemoration, this examination of the role of art in communicating religious truth was grandly enriched by a slide presentation of works that sadly cannot be shared here.

A final word. This volume of essays is affectionately dedicated to the memory of Michael Ramsey. For nearly a decade following his retirement from the see of Canterbury, Bishop Michael made Nashotah his home away from home, making annual visits to the House. During this time numerous American divinity students came to feel, as Isaac Williams once said of Keble, 'Each of us was always delighted to walk with him.' Indeed, he gave humble but commanding expression to the best in Anglicanism and to its catholicity, as did the country parson before him remembered in these essays. And we here at the House shall remain always thankful for his having reminded us of the high ideal of self-discipline and simplicity of life which has been our calling for over a century and a half now, but most importantly for giving us evidence of God's purpose in the renewal of heroic sanctity which we were privileged to behold in him. He crowned for us the catholic pilgrimage among Anglicans charted so long ago by Keble and his associates.

Charles R. Henery
Nashotah House
Transfiguration, 1994

Notes

1. *cf.*, 'The Rev. John Keble,' *The Church Review*, London, April 7, 1866, pp. 320–21; also, R.W. Church, *The Oxford Movement: Twelve Years, 1833–1845*, 3rd ed. (London: Macmillan and Co., 1892).

2. 'The Formal Resolutions of the Lambeth Conference of September 24–27, 1867' in *The Lambeth Conferences of 1867, 1878 and 1888*, ed. Randall T. Davidson (London: SPCK, 1889), 97.

3. W.H. Stowe, *The Life and Letters of Bishop William White* (New York: Morehouse, 1937), 269.

4. W.R.W. Stephens, *The Life and Letters of Walter Farquhar Hook* (London: R. Bentley & Son, 1880), 72–75; *British Critic*, 26 (October 1839): 334, 339.

5. *British Critic*, op. cit., 284*ff.*

6. Georgina Battiscombe, *John Keble, A Study in Limitations* (London: Constable, 1963), 103.

7. Letter of Benjamin I. Haight to William R. Whittingham, November 10, 1835, in the *Maryland Diocesan Archives*, Baltimore.

8. W.C. Doane, *A Memoir of the Life of George Washington Doane, Bishop of New Jersey* (New York: D. Appleton and Co., 1860), 283.

9. *The Mission of the Jubilee: Bishop DeLancey's Report to the Convention of the Diocese of Western New York* (Utica: Curtis & White, 1852), 17, 29.

10. Letter of Horatio Potter to the Clergy and Laity of the Diocese of New York, May 7, 1866, in the *Maryland Diocesan Archives*.

11. Doane, 259.

12. Letter of Arthur C. Coxe to B.I. Haight, May 15, 1866, in *The Murphey Collection*, no. 74, The General Theological Seminary, New York City. For a pioneering and valuable survey of Anglo-American church relations in the early 19th century, see Robert S. Bosher, *The American Church and the Formation of the Anglican Communion, 1823–1853* (Evanston: Seabury-Western Theological Seminary, 1962).

John Keble – A Speaking Life

I THE PRIEST

> Evangelical vicar in want
> Desires a portable font,
> Will exchange the same
> For a portrait in frame
> Of the bishop-elect of Vermont.

I begin with Ronald Knox's witty limerick because in these three essays I will seek to give a portrait of John Keble and assess important aspects of his significance. But portraits, as the limerick reminds us, should be in frames, and in John Keble's case we have the added difficulty of the subject. 'How', asked John Henry Newman, when asked to write on John Keble, 'can I profess to paint a man who will not sit for his portrait?' To that problem we will return, but let me begin by putting the portrait of Keble in its necessary frame.

We keep a bi-centenary of John Keble's birth. The day was April 25th, St. Mark's day; the year 1792. George III, one of the longest reigning of English monarchs had been thirty-two years on the throne, a reign which had already seen the American revolution and independence for Britain's American colonies. Another revolution, across the Channel in France, was already three years old and was the cause of mingled alarm and enthusiasm. Young Romantics could see France (and indeed America) as the harbinger of a new dawn, old oppressions swept away, a new order replacing the old. But the pulling down of the *ancien régime*, attacks on the monarchy and the established order, anti-clericalism and indeed attacks on Christianity: these forces unleashed by the revolution seemed to many on the English side of the Channel increasingly threatening. As the eighteenth century

1

drew to a close, there was no shortage of apocalyptic speculation. Students of biblical prophecy, accustomed to reading Daniel and Revelation as indictments of the papal antichrist wondered whether revolutionary France might not be as appropriate a candidate. It certainly reinforced a sense of British messianic mission when war was declared on Napoleon, the imperial successor to the revolutionaries. Throughout the first quarter of the nineteenth century British society was nervous of revolutionary ideas and social upheaval.

It was not only political ideas from France, that were troubling, there were the social changes consequent upon that other revolution, the industrial revolution, which was slowly but steadily changing the social face of Britain from a traditional, rural economy to a manufacturing one. The poet, Samuel Taylor Coleridge (who was also one of the most significant religious thinkers of the day), wrote that 'the smokes of our towns hide from us the face of heaven.' Not only was that literally the case – the pall of smoke from domestic fires and mill chimneys in the new northern industrial towns – it was also the sense that the new machinery was blocking out the vision of the world as God's creation. As with later technological revolutions, machines destroyed jobs. In reaction, in the Luddite riots, disaffected workers destroyed machines.

Fairford, in Gloucestershire, where John Keble was born, was far from the upheavals of the industrial revolution. It is not all that much changed today from what it would have been in 1792 when John Keble first saw the light of day in a tall Cotswold stone house, guarded from the Cirencester road by a high wall, a large cedar in the garden. His father, another John Keble, was priest of the neighbouring village of Coln St. Alwyn, but lived in his own accommodation in Fairford, riding or walking over to his parish to take the services and visit his parishioners. He lived into his nineties, and was still able to take the occasional service in extreme old age. Technically, because he lived outside his parish, he was a non-resident parish priest, and, as such, might have been marked down as contributing to the abuses of the Church of England by later zealous reformers. But he seems to have cared well and faithfully for his village parish, and doubtless John the younger learned much from him of pastoral and priestly duty.

The non-residence of John Keble senior is a reminder of that part of the portrait's frame which we must next consider: the condition of the Church of England through the years in which John Keble grew to manhood and led ultimately to that significant day in July 1833, when he preached the sermon before the judges of the Assize Court in Oxford, taking as his theme 'national apostasy,' the event which John Henry Newman marked as the beginning of the Oxford Movement.

England was a confessional state. Church and state were in theory viewed as two sides of a single coin. To sit in the House of Commons you had to be a member of the established church of England or of Scotland. To hold public office you had at the very least to conform occasionally to the Church of England by receiving the sacrament once a year. Dissenting congregations were tolerated, but lived under restrictions and disabilities. Roman Catholics suffered under penal laws, marking them as subjects whose loyalty was suspect because of allegiance to the pope, a foreign power, who had both 'no jurisdiction in this realm of England' (as the Thirty-Nine Articles put it), and who had excommunicated Elizabeth I in 1570, an action which seemed to brand all Roman Catholics as traitors. The folk memory of the Gunpowder Plot, marked with special services in the Book of Common Prayer, contributed to the anti-papal, no popery character of English popular religion. Another special service in the Prayer Book, that for the 30th January, marked the execution of Charles I in 1649. The Royal Martyr was venerated in particular by the High Church tradition, a tradition to which the Keble family belonged. John was brought up with a reverence for the martyr king, for the Stuart monarchy, and for the Nonjurors, who at the time of the 1688 revolution which expelled James II and brought in William and Mary had resigned their ecclesiastical offices rather than repudiate their oath of loyalty to the Stuarts. The departure of the Nonjurors had weakened the High Church tradition in the church, and the eighteenth century had seen a dominance of Latitudinarian divines, whose tepid religion and moralising sermons were frequently lacking in either a sense of mystery or the urgency of salvation.

Yet the High Church tradition had by no means disappeared. Recent scholarly work on the older High Churchmen in the thirty years or so preceding the Oxford Movement has shown them to be more powerful and influential than Oxford Movement historians would have us believe. In particular the group known as 'the Hackney Phalanx' was closely connected with Archbishops Charles Manners Sutton and William Howley. They revived the old missionary societies, the SPG (Society for the Propagation of the Gospel) and SPCK (Society for Promoting Christian Knowledge). They resisted the non-denominational religion of the Bible Society, urged liturgical decency, held a high sacramental doctrine and stressed apostolic succession. Newman's dedication of one of his works to Joshua Watson, one of the leading laymen of the Hackney Phalanx, is a reminder of the debt owed by the Tractarians to their predecessors. Bishop William Van Mildert of Durham was part of this group and considered John Keble for the post of principal of the newly founded Durham University.

The old High Churchmen of the Hackney Phalanx, whom the men of the Oxford Movement labelled the 'Zs', became increasingly concerned during the late 1820s and early 1830s as the constitutional situation of the Church of England was attacked and altered. The parliamentary union of England and Ireland in 1800 meant that Ireland's large Roman Catholic population, and its minority established Anglican church, now impinged directly on the British parliamentary process. There were pressures to remove the disabilities of Dissenters and to repeal the penal legislation governing Roman Catholics. Beyond that were proposals for the reform of Parliament. Each of these measures had a consequential effect on the Church of England. Bishops voting against such reforms brought the church into collision with government. The political catalyst of the Oxford Movement was the modification of the confessional state by the repeal of the Test and Corporation Acts, by Catholic Emancipation in 1829, and the Reform Bill of

1832. When the government moved to reform the Irish church establishment by the amalgamation of bishoprics, however justified this was on utilitarian grounds, to High Churchmen it was laying secular hands on sacred office. So the Irish Church Temporalities Bill provoked John Keble's 'decided protest' of 1833, his sermon on 'National Apostasy'. The identity of the Church of England was at stake. Newman recognised this in the question posed in the first of the *Tracts for the Times*, 'On what ground do you stand, O presbyter of the Church of England?'

Before turning to John Keble the priest, there are a few more details of the portrait's frame to note. The first is his family background. I have already spoken of his father. I must mention his mother, Sarah, the daughter of the rector of Ringwood in the New Forest, not so very far from Hursley where John Keble was to be parish priest for so much of his life, and not so very far from Bournemouth where he died in 1866. She, like John's father, was greatly loved by the family. There were four brothers and sisters to John. Elizabeth, the eldest, born in 1790, keen witted, devout and plagued by ill health throughout her life. Thomas, a year younger than John and close to him in religious views. He followed John to Oxford, and then as curate in Eastleach, and made his mark as vicar of Bisley in Gloucestershire. In 1827, the year he moved to Bisley, Thomas began the daily reading of the Offices in church (Matins at 10 a.m. and Evensong at 4 p.m.). The daily public recitation of the Office became a Tractarian hallmark, but was far from usual at the time. Thomas helped John with the edition of Hooker, the *Library of the Fathers* and the *Plain Sermons*. In 1838 John wrote, 'I was myself inclined to eclecticism at one time, and had it not been for my father and brother, where I should have been now who can say?'[1] There were two younger sisters, Sarah, who died young at eighteen in 1814, and Mary Anne, who also died prematurely at the age of twenty-five in 1826. It was a close-knit and happy family, and one marked by considerable intellectual ability. None of the children were sent away to school but were educated at home by their father. It was a good education (the boys learnt four languages) and it carried John to his place at Corpus Christi College in 1806 and on to his double first (in classics and mathematics) in 1810 when he was just eighteen. It was a result that marked John as a scholar of distinction. Only Robert Peel, later to become prime minister, had achieved such a result since the reform of the Oxford examinations in 1800.

So much for John Keble's family background, it remains only to outline briefly his life before we turn more specifically to look at Keble the priest. Following his success at Corpus Christi, he was elected to a fellowship at Oriel in April 1811, and so was brought into contact with the sharpest and most brilliant Oxford common room of the day, comprised of the group known as the Noetics, which included figures such as Edward Copleston, John Davison, Richard Whately and Edward Hawkins. He taught and examined in the Schools, and on Trinity Sunday 1815 he was ordained deacon, and priest a year later. As well as duties in college, he assisted his father in his village parishes, in particular looking after the two tiny Eastleach villages whose twin churches are a stone's throw apart, separated by a clear stream spanned by an old clapper bridge known to this day as Mr Keble's bridge. In 1823, following his mother's death, he became curate of Southrop, a couple of miles from Eastleach. His Oriel pupils came to Southrop for reading parties which formed their minds in a way which was formative for the Oxford Movement. In 1824 he declined an invitation from Bishop William Hart Coleridge to become archdeacon of Barbados, but in 1825 he spent a year at Hursley as deputy for the archdeacon of Winchester. He would have stayed longer there had it not been for the death of his youngest sister in 1826, which determined him to return to be with his father in Fairford, where he remained until his father's death in January 1835. That same year he married Charlotte Clarke and accepted appointment as vicar of Hursley, near Winchester, from his friend and former pupil, Sir William Heathcote, the squire of Hursley Park. Vicar of Hursley he remained until his death, though for ten years his Oxford connection was kept up in the part-time post of professor of poetry from 1831–41. He resigned his Oriel fellowship on his marriage, celibacy being then a requirement for fellows of Oxford and Cambridge colleges.

As will be evident from this short sketch of John Keble's life, it was not a life of high drama or great incident. His first biographer, his friend from Corpus Christi days, the lawyer Sir John T. Coleridge, warned his readers that they were 'about to enter on a most uneventful story.' 'Few persons have lived so long, and achieved so great a name, about whom there is little of change or incident to record. His life was passed in his father's house, in his college rooms, in his curacies, or in his vicarage, in occasional Long-Vacation rambles, in visits to the sea-side for alleviation of sickness. He earnestly avoided publicity; happily for himself perhaps, neither the Crown nor the church thought him a fit subject for promotion, which I need not say he never solicited, and I believe would have declined.'[2] Newman, as I have already mentioned, asked how it was possible to paint a portrait of a man who would not sit for his portrait. Georgina Battiscombe, whose biography of Keble was published in 1963, gave it a subtitle, 'a study in limitation.'[3] Henry Parry Liddon, preaching at the opening of Keble College Chapel in 1876, said 'no man ever lifted so many to heaven without mentioning it', than John Keble.[4] Edward Pusey, on the same occasion, said 'he was all prayer at all times, though those only who narrowly observed him saw it, and he knew not that it was observed; else he would have hid it.'[5]

There is a quality in Keble's personality, close to the heart of his priesthood, which is hidden and elusive. And it was this quality which made his life, for all its outward lack of incident, a 'speaking life', with a magnetic character to those who came in contact with it. It is worth pondering Pusey's sermon, for Pusey, who has himself been described as the *doctor mysticus* of the Oxford Movement, used Keble as his confessor and spiritual director. And it was Keble's wisdom which strove to make Pusey deal more lovingly and tenderly with himself in the dark days following the death of his wife, when morbid self-recrimination threatened to engulf him. Pusey chose as his text the beatitude, 'Blessed are the Meek'. The Beatitudes, he says, are the Lord's alphabet to be learned by his disciples. They belong together, and 'all imply some degree of self-denial, self-sacrifice or temporal hardness, willingly endured for the sake of God.'[6] Meekness is no exception. It is not easiness of disposition, sweetness of temper, kindliness, gentleness, nor kind-heartedness. It is, Pusey says, 'a grace formed by suffering', and in Hebrew 'afflicted, suffering, meek [and] humble are scarcely distinguishable.'[7] The meek are the humble, like the Blessed Virgin, who are exalted; they are those of patient endurance, and of deep penitence. The Lord described himself as 'meek and lowly of heart', and that same quality must be found in Christians, and above all in those called to Christian ministry. Pusey reminded his hearers how Keble had written that 'amid all our cheerful conversation, yea our mirth, we must keep down in our hearts a flow of serious earnest thought'; and that thought was of Christ and of souls.[8] 'The Passion of his Lord, Whom he loved,' wrote Pusey, 'was his book, his life', and it was this inner devotion which led Keble to adopt a rule, summer and winter, of being in church before dawn to pray for the church in her distress. Prayer was the weapon, not controversy. Pusey reminded his hearers in 1876, at a time when the Church of England was torn by the bitterness of the ritualist disputes: 'evil-speaking, mockery, sarcasm, lampooning, harsh censure, are not part of the armoury of God, nor "fruits of the Spirit".'[9]

When Keble was ordained deacon in 1815 he wrote to his friend, Coleridge:

> Pray for me, too; pray earnestly, my dear, my best friend, that He would give me His grace, that I may not be altogether unworthy of the sacred office, on which I am, rashly, I fear, even now entering. Pray that I may be freed from vanity, from envy, from discontent, from impure imaginations; that I may not grow weary, nor wander in heart from God's service; that I may not be judging others uncharitably, nor vainly dreaming how they will judge me, at the very moment that I seem most religiously and charitably employed. Without any foolish affectation of modesty, I can truly say that the nearer the time approaches, the more strongly I feel my own unfitness and unworthiness for the ministry; yet as I hope it is not such but that it

may be removed in time by earnest and constant use of the means of grace, I do not think it needful to defer my Ordination.[10]

A year later he again asked Coleridge's prayers. 'Every day I feel the dangers and anxieties of my profession increase upon me'.

Pray for me that I may not pollute God's altar with irregular, worldly-minded, self-complacent thoughts. Pray for me that I may free myself from all pride, all ambition, all uncharitableness.[11]

He remembered how Coleridge had cautioned him against formalism, and how that caution had struck home. 'I thought it hard at the time, but now I know you had too good reason — help me by your prayers, your advice ... and your reproof, if you at any time think I need it, to get rid of this dangerous habit.'[12]

Keble preached his first sermon a week after his ordination to the diaconate. It was the first Sunday after Trinity, and he took as his text words from the fourth chapter of the First Letter of John, part of the epistle for that Sunday: 'Beloved, if God so loved us, we ought also to love one another.' Both the theme and the sermon were appropriate to Keble. 'It is no high or secret thing which the Holy Ghost in this Scripture declares unto us,' he begins, 'but it is a word which is very nigh unto every one of us, even in our mouth and in our heart.' The fact that we have life and breath, reason and speech, body and soul, that we are 'fearfully and wonderfully made' is a declaration of God's loving providential care. God is our creator, redeemer and sanctifier, and the very pattern of our waking and sleeping is a reminder of the gift of life he has given us. The created order itself points to God. 'Take care that ye despise not God, nor forget Him, lest the very birds and beasts rise up in judgement against you. The dog fawns upon his own master, the redbreast hastens to the window where he is fed, the ox knoweth his owner, and the ass his master's crib: and shall not we know, and worship, and love, our Maker, our Saviour, our Teacher and Father?'[13]

Keble's father had passed on to his son a love of the great Anglican divines of the seventeenth century. When John and Tom had been undergraduates at Corpus Christi, they had spent some time in the archives investigating the records of perhaps the most famous theologian Corpus could claim, Richard Hooker, the author of the *Laws of Ecclesiastical Polity*. John was later to edit Hooker's works, and from these early years of his ordination there is a poem recording a visit to Hooker's grave at Bishopsbourne in Kent. That was in 1817. Two years later, in 1819, he made another pilgrimage to the tomb of another revered seventeenth-century divine, Henry Hammond. Hammond had been deprived of his living during the Commonwealth period, and this gave him something of the status of a confessor. Archbishop Henry R. McAdoo, in his study of Anglican theological method, emphasises Hammond's veneration for Ignatius of Antioch as a defender of episcopacy; Vincent of Lerins for his credal canon; and the important place given to the liturgy in the guardianship of apostolic faith – it was 'a hedge to keep out errors'. 'Learned in School-divinity, and a master in Church-antiquity, perfect and ready in the sense of the Fathers, Councils, ecclesiastical historians and liturgies', Hammond was a key theologian for Keble, as later for Newman.[14]

The erastian threat of legislation abolishing and amalgamating bishoprics in Ireland was the occasion of Keble's 1833 Assize Sermon, as that Assize Sermon was the symbolic point of departure for the Oxford Movement. The *Tracts for the Times* were planned as a rallying point for both clergy and laity, and as a means of bringing home the importance and significance of neglected doctrines. John Keble was the author of eight of the ninety *Tracts*.[15] The first of these, *Tract* 4, *ad populum* and priced at one penny, has for its title, 'Adherence to the Apostolical Succession the Safest Course.' It is, says Keble, 'a high privilege, that we belong to an Apostolic Church', and it is a matter of deep regret 'that so many of us are, almost avowedly, so cold and indifferent in our thoughts of this privilege.' The cause of this in part is, he suggests, 'the comparatively low ground which we ourselves, the Ministers of God, have chosen to occupy in defence of our commission. For many years, we have been much in the habit of resting our claim on the general duties of submission to authority, of decency and order, of respecting precedents long established; instead of appealing to that warrant, which marks us, *exclusively*, for GOD'S AMBASSADORS.' The tone has been much the same as if priests had been 'mere Laymen, acting for ecclesiastical purposes by a commission under the Great Seal.' 'Silently and insensibly' the high ground taken by the bishops and presbyters of the primitive church had been abandoned. The ground of that principle was, Keble suggests, a eucharistic one. 'The Holy Feast on our SAVIOUR's sacrifice, which all confess to be "generally necessary to salvation", was intended by Him to be constantly conveyed through the hands of commissioned persons.' Unless such a warrant is clearly evident we cannot be 'sure that our hands convey the sacrifice.' Not only good order, but 'Piety', 'Christian Reverence, and sincere and devout Love of our Redeemer,' and 'Charity to the souls of our brethren' would 'prompt us, at all earthly risks, to preserve and transmit the seal and warrant of CHRIST.' It makes a difference if the doctrine of the ministry is thought of as a 'mere voluntary ecclesiastical arrangement,' or is traced 'to our LORD'S own institution.'

'JESUS CHRIST'S own commission,' he continues, 'is the best external security I can have, that in receiving this bread and wine, I verily receive His Body and Blood. Either the Bishops have that commission, or there is no such thing in the world.' The principles of High Churchmanship are implicit in Paul's words, 'Let a man so account of us, as of the Ministers of CHRIST, and Stewards of the mysteries of God.' It was a diminishment of the gospel to 'talk so much of an *Establishment*, and so little of an APOSTOLICAL SUCCESSION.' Keble passes no judgement on Roman Catholics or Presbyterians, for 'necessary to salvation' and 'necessary to Church Communion' are not convertible terms. 'It is our business to keep fast hold of the Church Apostolical ... not merely on civil or ecclesiastical grounds, but from real personal love and reverence, affectionate reverence to our LORD and SAVIOUR.'

The doctrine of the apostolic ministry is, Keble continues, 'part of that ineffable mystery, called in our Creed, The Communion of Saints; and with all other Christian mysteries, is above the *understanding* of all alike, yet *practically* alike within reach of all.' This re-affirmation of the theology of mystery is one of the key Tractarian themes. Newman, in *Tract* 73, on 'The Introduction of rationalistic Principles into Religion,' reminded his readers that the terms 'Revelation' and 'Mystery' were not antithetical. The God of revelation was also a hidden God. His very transcendence and our human finitude meant that his revelation was by 'economy' and dispensation, an accommodation to the weakness of our human intellect. Christianity was not only wrongly characterised as 'not mysterious', it was 'necessarily mysterious'. Pusey, in his unpublished 'Lectures on Types and Prophecies,' lumped Evangelical sloganisers, rationalising divines, and dogmatic over-systematisers together as lacking in true humility before the mystery of God. For him both the denial of the Real Presence and transubstantiation as an explanation of that Presence were symptomatic of the same failing. It was not for nothing that Newman told the Evangelical Sir James Stephen that Christians 'receive the gospel literally on their knees', indicating a different habit of mind from that argumentative spirit which sitting and listening engendered. To see the ministry of the church, and the church itself, as part of the mystery of the communion of Saints, would have a transforming effect on the understanding of the relationship of priest and people, or, as Keble puts it, 'Pastor and Parishioner'.

Look on your pastor as acting by man's commission, and you may respect the authority by which he acts, you may venerate and love his personal character, but it can hardly be called a *religious* veneration; there is nothing, properly, *sacred* about him. But once learn to regard him as 'the Deputy of CHRIST, for reducing man to the obedience of GOD;' and every thing about him becomes changed, every thing stands in a new light. In public and in private, in church and at home, in consolation and

in censure, and above all, in the administration of the
Holy Sacraments, a faithful man naturally considers,
'By this His messenger CHRIST is speaking to me;
by his very being and place in the world, he is a
perpetual witness to the truths of the sacred history,
a perpetual earnest of Communion with our LORD to
those who come duly prepared to His Table.' In short,
it must make just all the difference in every part of a
Clergyman's duty, whether he do it, and be known to
do it, in that Faith of his commission from CHRIST,
or no.[16]

The theme of the apostolic ministry is continued in *Tract
52*, in the form of a sermon for the Feast of St. Matthias.
Keble notes that St. Luke, at the beginning of the Acts of the
Apostles, refers to Jesus before his Ascension, 'speaking of
the things pertaining to the Kingdom of God.' He then notes
that the nature of that instruction is not recorded. 'Instead
of finding any report of *what our blessed* SAVIOUR *said*,
we find a report of *what His Apostles did*;' an indication
'that we must look to *the actual conduct and system of the
early Church* for a true notion of the things pertaining to 'the
kingdom of God.' The first of those things is the ordination of
Matthias, which shows, Keble argues, two points: 'First . . .
that whoever are regularly commissioned by the Apostles,
our LORD will consider those persons as commissioned and
ordained by Himself. Secondly, it proves that such power to
ordain is independent of those apostolical functions, which
may be properly called extraordinary and miraculous' (i.e. it
preceded Pentecost). Indeed, Keble goes so far as to suggest
that the Lord 'purposely abstained from nominating St.
Matthias in His life-time, in order that Christians in all
times might understand that the ordained successors of the
Apostles are as truly Bishops under Him, as ever the Apostles
were themselves.' An all too prevalent error, Keble goes on,
'is that of imagining that Church communion is a voluntary
thing' and that 'Christian ministry is also a voluntary thing;
that there is no real difference between clergy and laity, any
more than is enacted by the law of the land for mere decency
and order's sake; but that otherwise a man who can and

will do good as a clergyman, is to all intents and purposes clergyman enough.'

By contrast the doctrine of the church traces the apostolicity of its ministry back to Christ himself, 'the chief Shepherd and Bishop,' who commissions the apostles and through them the bishops. 'Therefore, although there be many Bishops, yet the Episcopal office is but one.' The bishops were 'the connecting chain which bound the successive generations of Christians to the first generation' so that to break off connections with the apostles was to break off connection with Christ. Keble calls as a witness to this understanding Ignatius of Antioch.

> 'The teaching of the Primitive Church brought this matter home to every man's own soul, not only on the general ground of submission to all our Lord's ordinances, but because the bread and wine in the Eucharist was not accounted the true Sacrament of CHRIST, without CHRIST's warrant given to the person administering ... In the judgment of the Church, the Eucharist administered without apostolical commission, may to pious minds be a very edifying ceremony, but it is not that blessed thing which our SAVIOUR graciously meant it to be: it is not "verily and in deed taking and receiving" the Body and Blood of Him, our Incarnate LORD.' So, Keble concludes, 'Communion with GOD incarnate, such Communion as He offers in His holy Supper, cannot be depended on without an Apostolical Ministry.'

Tract 54, a sermon for the Annunciation, fills out the theme of apostolic ministry, concentrating not on the commission to celebrate the eucharist, but on the teaching office. 'From the time of our LORD, the Apostolical succession of pastors has continued, as a divinely-appointed guard, meant to secure the integrity of Apostolical doctrine.' In the ancient church, he suggests, 'episcopal anathemas' were 'the Church's main safeguard against the misinterpretations of Scripture.' In recent times, wherever apostolic succession is lacking 'the true doctrine of our LORD's incarnation has been often corrupted, always in jeopardy.' Irenaeus's appeal to the apostolic doctrine taught by the succession of public teachers in the great sees in his battle with the gnostics; the controversy between Dionysius of Rome and Dionysius of Alexandria, and the condemnation of Paul of Samosata are all cited in support of the episcopal teaching office in the early Church. The second point, concerning lack of apostolic ministry and heterodox doctrine, is pursued by Keble in *Tract* 57, a sermon for St. Mark's day, preached on Ephesians 4.14: 'That we henceforth be no more children, tossed to and fro, and carried about with every wind of doctrine.' It echoes in a measure the line taken by Hugh James Rose in his critique of German theology, in which he laid the blame for German theological rationalism at the door of Lutheran and Reformed ministries lacking the apostolic succession.[17] Keble cites a passage from Tertullian in which he complains about contemporary heretics who sit lightly to church order.

> Their Catechumens become complete Christians before they have quite learned their lessons ... *Their ordinations are off-handed, light, variable* ... mere novices are raised by them to Church office, sometimes men engaged in worldly business ... Accordingly one man shall be their Bishop today, another to-morrow, to-day a Deacon, to-morrow a reader; to-day a Presbyter, to-morrow a mere layman. *For in laymen also they will vest the powers and functions of the Priesthood.*

Turning to more recent times, Keble surveys the doctrinal state of churches which have dispensed with the episcopal succession: the Lutherans of North Germany; the Reformed churches of Switzerland, Holland and Scotland; and Congregationalist churches in England and America. In Germany rationalist and deistical theology had, Keble judged, made greater inroads than in England, though England was the source of many of the ideas. In England the Presbyterian churches had all but embraced Unitarianism. Among Congregationalists Keble judges there to be a 'systematical disparagement of the holy Sacraments,' a 'horror ... of authority and antiquity,' and a 'tendency ... to make Faith a matter of *feeling* rather than a strict relative duty towards the persons of the HOLY TRINITY.' As to American Congregationalism Keble quotes a Unitarian writer: 'In the United States, where there are no obstructions to the progress of knowledge and truth, the spread of liberal doctrines has exceeded our most sanguine expectations.' 'The only country, therefore, of Christendom where congregational principles of *government* entirely prevail, is likewise the only country which witnesses the rapid and unmitigated growth of Unitarian principles of *doctrine*.' Reverence for apostolic faith and order and deference for those who succeeded to the apostolic commission is, Keble concludes, an important safeguard for the doctrine of the Incarnation.

What Keble writes in the *Tracts* is drawn out in the sermon on 'Primitive Tradition', which he preached in Winchester Cathedral in September 1836, and in some of his comments in his long preface to his edition of Hooker's *Works* (1841). It is tradition which supplies 'the system and arrangement of fundamental Articles' of the faith, notably the Creeds; it guides the church in the interpretation of Scripture; and it is a further guide in practical matters, 'the discipline, formularies, and rites of the Church of Christ.' The canon of Scripture, the doctrines of the Trinity and Incarnation, the pattern of the eucharist, and apostolic succession are, declares Keble, 'the points of Catholic consent known by tradition' which 'constitute the knots and ties of the whole system.' Preaching on the text from II Timothy 1.14: 'That good thing which was committed unto thee keep by the Holy Ghost which dwelleth in us;' Keble maintains that 'the obvious meaning of the text is, that the treasure of sound doctrine was to be guarded by the grace of the Apostolical Succession'. Where the succession fails the truth is in jeopardy. Those who are called by their ordination to guard the faith, must beware of 'the fatal error of treating theology like any human science, as a subject in which every succeeding age might be expected to advance on the former.' In the early church the threat was gnosticism. Keble suggests that in his own day the threat was a variety of nominalism; 'I mean, the habit of resolving the high mysteries of the faith into mere circumstances of language, methods of speaking adapted to our weak understandings, but with no real counterpart in the nature of things.'[18] Keble is alert to the problem, as we would call it, of cultural relativism. He does not deny that history shapes langauge; he is more concerned that the Christian theologian recognises the treasure given by the Spirit of God in these earthen vessels. In his preface to Hooker, Keble notes that the writings of the Fathers portray a sense of Christians being those who live in a new heaven and a new earth. Ordinary things become means of grace, pledges and tokens of God's presence and favour; they are capable of becoming *mysteria* or sacraments. The mystical interpretation of Scripture, ritual and ceremonial, and the church as a place of supernatural blessing were all part of this same understanding. Theology was a theology of mystery, and Christian life was a participation in a supernatural mystery. 'Clearness and symmetry of doctrine' are, Keble says, 'a dear purchase, when Christian truth and duty must be impaired for their sake. After all, a fragment of the true Temple is worth all the palaces of modern philosophical theology.'[19] In the lived mystery of the Christian life, the ordained three-fold ministry has a special place; and Keble underlines Hooker's high understanding of ordination, quoting from the fifth book of the *Laws of Ecclesiastical Polity*: 'Whether we preach, pray, baptize, communicate, condemn, give absolution, or whatever as disposers of God's mysteries; our words, judgments, acts and deeds, are not ours, but the Holy Ghost's ... The power of the ministry of God translateth out of darkness into glory; it raiseth men from the earth, and bringeth God Himself down from heaven; by blessing visible elements, it maketh them invisible grace; it giveth daily the Holy Ghost.'[20] Hooker, says Keble, 'made no question as to the mystical import and virtue of the form, wherewith the Church of England ordains and consecrates,' though he avoided the error that 'grace implies infallibility.'[21]

Towards the end of his life, in 1864, two years before he died, Keble was invited to preach at the anniversary of Bishop Samuel Wilberforce's theological college at Cuddesdon. It was Pentecost, and he took as his theme 'Pentecostal Fear,' preaching on the text from Acts 2.23: 'And fear came upon every soul.' Like Lancelot Andrewes before him, he sees Pentecost, 'God in us,' as the fulfilment of the Incarnation, 'God with us.' 'In Him they now live by a new life, which they have entirely from Him; a life which is both His and theirs, whereby they are so joined to Him as to be verily and indeed "partakers of a Divine nature".' The Whitsun glory was so high and inconceivable that the Fathers called it deification. The Pentecostal church is marked not only by the apostolic creed, ministry, eucharist and prayers, it also has the mark of Pentecostal fear. 'It is the greatness, the constant presence, the divinity of the unspeakable Gift by which every duty is done, which causes the duty to become so great and awful, and which throngs the whole of a man's course alike with glorious opportunities and exceeding dangers.' It is not slavish fear of which Keble speaks, but 'intense unspeakable adoration, a bowing down to the Light unapproachable, the Presence of which no creature can be worthy.' The Pentecostal gift is 'a Divine enrapturing awe.' It is a gift which 'will go up with them into heaven, and with its twin grace, the love of God, now made perfect, will be part of their happiness for ever.'[22] We are to live in a supernatural state.

To live 'in a supernatural state, full of Divine wonders' is the special responsibility of the priest and pastor. So Keble addresses the clergy and ordinands in his congregation:

> One man goes about his parish with the ever-present belief, that both he, and every one whom he meets, has the Holy Spirit within him — both he and they by Holy Baptism, he also, in a peculiar sense, by Holy Orders. Another, perhaps no less earnest in work, is mainly taken up with natural and social differences. One goes into a church, thinks of Isaiah's vision, says to himself, 'Here is the Lord sitting on His throne, high and lifted up, and His glory filling the place: here are the angels, hither Christ cometh in His Sacraments.' To another the place is nothing mysterious; he thinks only of edification and comfortable prayer ... must we not own that such a one, how good and sincere soever, is hardly great-hearted enough for his condition and privileges?
>
> Other instances each one may easily imagine for himself and surely, my brethren, the experience of each of us will tell him that in such measure as he

has tried and prayed, with fear and trembling, to keep up his high sense of the continued Pentecostal Gift, so far he has found his ministry blessed, with whatever disappointment in the visible results. That faith has been to him, as it will be to all who will prove it, worth all other motives and helps put together.[23]

That surely brings us very near the heart of John Keble the priest, who rose before dawn every morning to pray for the church of God, and by whose speaking life many were taught the meaning of priesthood, prayer and holiness.

Notes

1. Walter Lock, *John Keble: A Biography*, 5th ed. (London: Methuen, 1893), 3.
2. John T. Coleridge, *Memoir of the Rev. John Keble, M.A., Late Vicar of Hursley*, 3rd ed., (Oxford: J. Parker, 1870), 3.
3. Georgina Battiscombe, *John Keble: A Study in Limitations* (New York: Alfred A. Knopf, 1964), xviii–xix.
4. Henry P. Liddon, 'John Keble: Preached at Keble College, Oxford, on occasion of the opening of the Chapel and laying the Foundation-Stone of the Hall and Library on the Feast of St. Mark, April 25, 1876,' in *Clerical Life and Work: A Collection of Sermons, with an Essay* (London: Longmans, 1894), 353.
5. Edward B. Pusey, *Blessed Are The Meek: A Sermon Preached at the Opening of the Chapel of Keble College on St. Mark's Day, 1876* (Oxford: J. Parker, 1876), 26.
6. *Ibid.*, 4.
7. *Ibid.*, 5.
8. *Ibid.*, 26–27.
9. *Ibid.*, 27.
10. Coleridge, *Memoir*, 58.
11. *Ibid.*, 59.
12. *Ibid.*, 59.
13. John Keble, *Sermons, Occasional and Parochial* (Oxford: J. Parker, 1868), 27.
14. Henry R. McAdoo, *The Spirit of Anglicanism: A Survey of Anglican Theological Method in the Seventeenth Century* (New York: Scribner, 1965), 358–68.
15. *Tract* Nos. 4, 13, 40, 52, 54, 57, 60, 89.
16. *Tract* No. 4. It is characteristic of Keble's contribution to the *Tracts*, and indicative of his own understanding, that he uses the word 'pastor' in a way that his fellow contributors do not.

17. Pusey, in his response to Rose, dissented from this. At this stage in his theological development Pusey saw the weakness in the divorce of spirituality from theology and looked to the pietist tradition to redress the balance. See E.B. Pusey, *An Historical Inquiry into the Probable Causes of the Rationalist Character Lately Predominant in the Theology of Germany*. (London: C. and J. Rivington, 1828).

18. Keble, 'Primitive Tradition Recognized in Holy Scripture,' in *Sermons, Academical and Occasional* (Oxford: J.H. Parker, 1847), 173–220.

19. Keble, 'Postscript to the Sermon on Tradition' in *Sermons, Academical and Occasional*, 357.

20. *Ibid.*, 374.

21. *Ibid.*, 374–75.

22. J. Keble, *Pentecostal Fear: A Sermon Preached in the Parish Church, Cuddesdon, on Tuesday, May 24, 1864, on the Anniversary of the Theological College*. (Oxford: J. Parker, 1864), 7–8, 15–17, 21–22.

23. *Ibid.*, 27.

II THE PASTOR

In the *Tracts for the Times* of which John Keble was the author, it is characteristic of him to use the word 'pastor' of Christian ministry more frequently than his fellow authors. This is not surprising, for Keble has passed into Anglican history as one of the great exemplars of the parish priest. This is partly because he did not seek promotion and chose to spend almost his entire ministry in small rural communities, first as a curate in Gloucestershire and then as vicar of Hursley in the diocese of Winchester. The setting of his ministry, rather than his being the author of treatises on parochial ministry and pastoral care, has coloured the tradition. A certain romanticism has also entered in, with Keble the country parish priest being the exemplar of that rather idyllic picture of the parish priest of the English village which belongs to a certain kind of Anglican mythology. Professor Owen Chadwick gave us a picture in his book, *Victorian Miniature*, of a Norfolk village where parochial life was characterised by tension between parson and squire. Hursley was different. Keble's patron, and former pupil, Sir William Heathcote, who lived in the great house, Hursley Park, just up the drive from Keble's church and vicarage, was his strong supporter. And Keble enjoyed close relationships with some of the Winchester notables, particularly the headmaster of William of Wykeham's ancient foundation, Winchester College, George Moberly, who rented a country property in Keble's parish.

If Keble did not write a treatise on pastoral practice, he, like his brother Thomas at Bisley in Gloucestershire, was concerned that his parish should be run on church principles and exemplify Tractarian priorities. He gave encouragement to those who did write on pastoral matters, men like Edward Monro of Harrow Weald. He was concerned, as many Victorians were, with the proper provision of church buildings, and built new churches for his outlying villages at Ampfield and Otterbourne, and completely rebuilt Hursley church, incorporating in it a sequence of windows not dissimilar to the magnificent mediaeval sequence he had known as a boy in the parish church of Fairford.

But there is more to Keble's pastoral reputation than his very English rural setting. There was, of course, the man himself and his combination of sharp intellect with a reserve and humility which were so central to his character. I have already referred to Newman's comment, 'How can I profess to paint the portrait of a man who will not sit?' If we would know Keble the pastor, we need first to sense the kind of impact he made on those who encountered him and try to sense what manner of man it was who throughout his life found people coming to seek his advice and counsel.

In her book, *Dulce Domum*, published in 1916, Catherine Moberly endeavoured to correct the rather milk-and-water picture of Keble. She wrote: 'Mr. Keble's sensitive shrinking from anything like praise and observation has perhaps been the cause for the idea gaining ground that he was rather a gentle, holy man than a strong living force in church matters. His friends, on the contrary, remember chiefly the fiery eagerness, the indignant remonstrances poured out, and the sternness of his judgment when he thought church doctrine was being endangered. Eagle-eyed to detect danger, he allowed no one to be idle if things could be better by letters or protests.' At the time of the controversy over the theological liberalism of *Essays and Reviews* (1861), Keble issued a 'Litany of our Lord's Warnings' to ward against disbelief in hell. Miss Moberly cites a newspaper article in *The Guardian* as an admirable description of Keble.

Homely plainness, in manner, in speech, in the external aspect and practice of his religious life, went along in singular combination with rich and delicate cultivation, with fire of imagination, with the loftiest thoughts and an ever-present consciousness of the unseen. His horror was – it was almost morbid, but that it was so genuine and consistent – to allow the consciousness to come into his mind of his gifts and success, or to do anything which looked like setting them to advantage. He absolutely revolted at the least thought of display. And so in intercourse with strangers, or in his writings, in his preaching, the first feeling was of disappointment; he seemed dry, hard, awkward even – a contrast to all that had perhaps been suggested by 'The Christian Year'; there was indeed something more, not to be missed, of strange sweetness, of refined considerateness, or curious downright force and strength, which somehow mingled, one knew not how with what seemed unattractive, or flashed up and drove it at once out of sight: the evidence of the power, the grace and beauty of soul, the deep and living religion was not on the outside, and for the superficial and unreal might not be found at all. The plain, retiring, shy country-bred Englishman, jealous of everything brilliant and on his guard against everything hollow, masked to common eyes at once the poet and the saint.[1]

There are other descriptions which fill out this picture. A pupil of Keble's commented that 'we undergraduates used to think him, for a little man, which he was, a very well-made man.' It was the fashion then for men to wear tight pantaloons, which showed the figure. He also played a very good knife and fork at table, though always a most temperate man.[2] Another witness known only by initials – M.T. (perhaps Maria Trench) – described him in the following terms.

Mr. Keble was of middle height, the shoulders not rounded, and in fact almost square, but extremely low, which made him look shorter than he was, his arms very long and all limbs looking as if they were somewhat loosely hung ... His head, foreheard, eyes and hair, were fine even as to outward appearance, the head exquisitely formed, very straight behind and covered with perfectly white hair, soft and thick; the forehead *very* broad, strong and smooth ... the eyes hazel, and beautifully shaped, but it is impossible to describe them, or the rich depth of their colour and light. They used to shine like no other eyes, at times also flashing ... and at others sparkling with pleasure and humour ... The first impression ... of his whole person and air is that of a most singular simplicity and artlessness.[3]

Short-sighted, preferring standing to sitting, writing busily on scraps of paper at his standing-desk or the mantelpiece, while friends and visitors chatted around him; rapidly reading a book, sniffing out its sense, with spectacles pushed up on his forehead and the book held uncomfortably close to his face; an affection for and delight in children, matched by his own simplicity – all of these characteristics are noted by those who knew him well.

His own theology and pastoral practice had been shaped by his father. 'The highest praise which he seemed able to give to any theological statement was, "It seems to me just what my father taught me."'[4] He continued to use morning and evening the family prayers of Bishop Thomas Wilson of Sodor and Man (whose life he was later to write). These morning prayers begin with sentences read by 'one of the Family that can read' saying devoutly:

> The Lord hath brought us safe to the beginning of this day; let us, therefore, give thanks for this, and for all his mercies.
> Let us pray that we may live in the fear of God; and continue in love and charity with our neighbours.
> That his Holy Spirit may direct and rule our hearts, teach us what we ought to do, and what to avoid:
> That the grace of God may ever be with us to support us in all danger, and carry us through all temptations:
> That the Lord may bless all our honest endeavours, and make us content with what his providence shall order for us:
> And that we may continue his faithful servants this day, and unto our lives' end.
> For all which blessings let us devoutly pray.
> *Then all devoutly kneeling, let one say,*
>
> O GOD, by whom the whole world is governed and preserved, we give thee humble thanks for thy fatherly care over us, beseeching thee to make us truly sensible of thy mercies, and thankful for them.
> Give us grace that we many walk as in thy sight, making a conscience of our ways; and, fearing to

offend thee, may never fall into the sins we have repented of.

Enable us to resist the temptations of the world, the flesh, and the devil; to *follow* the motions of thy good Spirit; to be *serious* and *holy* in our lives; *true* and *just* in our dealings; *watchful* over our thoughts, words, and actions; *diligent* in our business: and *temperate in all things.*

May thy blessing be upon our persons, upon our labours, upon our substance, and upon all that belongs to us!

Give us grace that we may honestly improve all the talents which thou has committed to our trust; and that no worldly business, no worldly pleasures, may divert us from the thoughts of the life to come.

Make us sensible and thankful for all thy favours; and mindful of the wants of others.

By thy mighty power defend us in all the assaults of our enemies; and grant that this day we fall into no sin, neither run into any kind of danger; but that all our doings may be ordered by thy governance, to do always that which is righteous in thy sight.

May our gracious God give us what is needful for us, and grace not to abuse his favours; and withal, give us contented minds!

Give us in this world the knowledge of his truth, and in the world to come life everlasting. *Amen.*

Hear us, O God, not according to our weak understandings, but according to the full meaning of that *form of prayer* which Jesus Christ has taught us.

The version of these family prayers published by the SPCK concludes with *A Short and Plain Instruction for the True understanding of the Lord's Supper, with the Necessary Preparation Required for the Benefit of Young Communicants, and of such as have not well considered this Holy Ordinance* – a work with which John Keble is also likely to have been familiar.[5]

Keble recommended an ordinand to read, mark and learn from Butler's *Analogy of Religion*, Pearson's *Commentary on the Creed*, and Hooker's *Laws of Ecclesiastical Polity*. It was from Keble, Newman tells us in his *Apologia*, that he learned both Butler's maxim 'probability the guide of life' and a strong sense of sacramentalism, the former helping to shape the understanding of the relationship of faith and reason which he was to develop in his *University Sermons* and later in *The Grammar of Assent*. When Keble prepared the novelist Charlotte Yonge for confirmation, he went through the Prayer Book liturgies for baptism, confirmation and the eucharist, comparing them step by step with the earlier liturgies, working from William Palmer's *Origines Liturgicae*, and translating from the Greek. It was a very unusual and high-powered confirmation class.

If Keble was absent from Oxford for the greater part of his ministry, he was certainly not absent from the controversies of the day. He took a full part in the eucharistic controversies surrounding the archdeacon of Taunton, George Anthony Denison, and came to the defence of the first Tractarian bishop, Alexander Penrose Forbes of Brechin, who was arraigned by the bishops of the Episcopal Church of Scotland for his eucharistic teaching and his defence of the old Scottish Communion Office. His advice was sought by many who wrote him letters or came to seek his counsel at Hursley.

This aspect of his pastoral ministry may be seen in the *Letters of Spiritual Counsel and Guidance*, edited by his former curate R.F. Wilson. In his preface Wilson suggests that Keble's letters have a certain resemblance to those of Fénelon and St. Francis de Sales, more especially the latter – a saint whom Newman also thought that Keble resembled. Wilson also notes how Keble's strong sense of humility and self-depreciation is such a marked characteristic of these letters. Keble would, we may surmise, have shrunk from the description that he was a 'spiritual *director*', however much he would have had a strong sense of the authority and divine commission of priesthood. 'You could hardly,' Wilson writes, 'ask his opinion on a matter of any difficulty, on which his advice would not be given with this sort of hesitancy; so much so, as sometimes to leave persons uncertain what he really meant to counsel or direct, or whether he had made up his own mind in the matter.' Furthermore, Wilson goes on, 'this manner resulted not simply from most rare personal humility: there was another element underlying and prompting this humility, — a deep sense of personal unworthiness and sinfulness, finding utterance sometimes in expressions of self-abasement and self-condemnation, so strong, as quite to startle and distress one.'[6] As an example, Wilson cites a sermon in which Keble draws out the overwhelming awe we ought to feel if the doctrine of the indwelling of the Spirit is taken with full seriousness. If we are indeed 'the Temple of God, and ... the Spirit of God dwelleth in us: this, indeed, is awful beyond all awfulness.' And Wilson goes on to make an interesting connection between Keble's sense of penitence and acknowledgement of sin, and his theory of poetry as the 'irrepressible expression of pent-up feelings, which crave for utterance.' 'Poetry becomes a sort of public confession of what is within, though veiled by being generalized.'[7]

Let us now look to Keble as an exponent of practical religion, as his generation would have called it. He urges someone with a melancholic self-obsession 'to go out and do something kind to somebody or other.' 'Objects either rich or poor will generally present themselves in the hour of need to those who look for them in earnest, although Oxford is not perhaps the most convenient place to find them in.'[8] 'Do not indulge in remorse as a matter of feeling or fancy. There is none of us but has reason enough to make himself miserable in that way, if it were at all allowable to do so.'[9] A correspondent is concerned about the strictness of Christ's teaching. Keble replies, the misgivings are 'perfectly right and reasonable — and the more you allow them, *in a quiet way*, to influence you in practice, the happier and wiser you will be.' The strict sayings of Jesus should be viewed not as tasks, or conditions for entering heaven, but as *'friendly advice* ... practices and tempers of mind, naturally and reasonably flowing from what we know to be the truth of our condition, and of God's dealings with us.'[10] Keble commends William Law's *Serious Call to a Devout and Holy Life* and his *Treatise on Christian Perfection*. In a following letter he says that Law ought to be read 'with great caution, lest one should delight one's self so much with the ingenuity and eloquence of the writer as to forget that 'tis a very practical book.' Law, Keble says, needs to be modified and tempered by a writer such as Bishop Wilson. Law is too apt to take the line that because things can be abused they ought to be given up altogether. Keble is for a wise and tolerant moderation.[11] Keble, though strong for discipline, is always concerned for a true joy and cheerfulness in religion. 'He who takes the injunction "do all to the glory of God," in the most literal sense, appears to me to come nearest to the true sense of it. But ... I do not think the glory of God best promoted by a rigid abstinence from amusements, except they be either sinful in themselves, or carried to excess, or in some other way ministering occasion to sin.'[12]

To another correspondent, a priest, Keble writes, 'all my life long, I have been used to take what many would call the *laxer* view of common recreations and the ordinary pleasures of life.' The Bible itself, besides being the Word of God, gives many 'secondary satisfactions' – poetry, language and history, ... 'its blessings on conjugal love, family delights, the ways of little children, the beauties and mysteries of art and nature.' 'It seems to say, "Take all these and make much of them, for God's glory: be assured that there is nothing innocent so trifling, that it may not be thus sacrificed to Him."'[13]

> The trivial round, the common task,
> Will furnish all we ought to ask;
> Room to deny ourselves, a road.
> To bring us daily nearer God.[14]

Such a course, he suggests, is recommended by the greatest Anglican writers, such as Hooker, Jeremy Taylor, George Herbert and Izaak Walton. To a bereaved father he writes of the comfort to be gained from the ancient church of the knowledge that 'we may innocently and piously pray for our departed, and that they no doubt remember and pray for us,' and he commends Lancelot Andrewes commemoration of the departed in his *Preces Privatae*.[15] To another he encourages the use of eucharistic devotions from the ancient liturgies, for which there was Anglican precedent in the devotional works of Bishops Andrewes and Wilson. Conduct is not to be measured by feeling — 'This is the love of God, that we keep his commandments.' 'Our conduct He leaves to ourselves, but our feelings He keeps, in great measure, in His own Hands.'[16] To make sensible comfort and assurance a 'sure or necessary sign of God's favour, *must* be a mistake, if it were only that it contradicts the Lord's agony and the feeling that he had on the Cross.' The peace of God is 'too high and blessed a gift to be tested and analysed by any emotions, or by any reasoning of ours. The holy writers seem rather to speak of it as a kind of instinct, like infants' trust in their mothers, than as of a definite feeling or view, which we can experience or reflect upon.'[17] In many letters, particularly ones which seem to refer to sin in sexual relations, Keble stresses the need to avoid occasions of sin: 'In this war flying is better soldiership than fighting.'[18] Distractions in prayer may be met 'by mechanical helps — something equivalent to a Rosary.' 'And you will remember Bishop Taylor's advice, to gather up as it were all the meaning of the lost prayer into a hearty Amen at the end of it.'[19]

There is advice for those on the eve of ordination:

Take the word of one who knows, by sad experience, that there is no comfort for an ordained person, but in really striving, night and day, to keep his Ordination vows, and especially that one, in which we bind ourselves to frame and fashion our lives according to the doctrine of Christ ... Take my word for it, your first and chief business will be to keep yourself in order: I mean, especially, your senses and thoughts; if they be duly guarded, all the rest will be blessed; if they be duly indulged and let to run wild, you may do much good, and seem exemplary, yet all will be poisoned and blighted within, and if you are saved, it will be so as by fire.

The priest before putting his hand to the Ark must be a true penitent. 'Do not forget,' writes Keble, 'to befriend and pray for yourself.'[20]

One of the major themes of Keble's letters is his stress on the importance of sacramental confession. An undated letter speaks of how the parish is taking up more and more of his time. As acquaintance with people grew, so pastoral opportunities multiplied, but Keble was convinced that 'we go on working in the dark ... until the rule of systematic Confession is revived in our Church ... we are in our parishes like people whose lantern has blown out, and who are feeling their way, and continually stepping in puddles and splotches of mud, which they think are dry stones.' Justification by faith had been so distorted as to remove a sense of the reality of sin. 'The idea of Protestantism,' he writes, 'seems inseparable to me from "Every man his own absolver;" that is, in other words, the same as "Peace where there is no peace," and mere shadows of Repentance.'[21] He advises a correspondent preparing to make a general confession to consult Jeremy Taylor's *Holy Dying* and *The Golden Grove*, as well as Kettlewell's *Companion to the Penitent*. (John Kettlewell, the Nonjuring incumbent of Coleshill in Warwickshire, compiled forms of self-examination, confession and absolution, which were highly regarded by Archbishop William Wake at the beginning of the eighteenth century, as well as by Keble in the nineteenth). Keble is a wise confessor. He advises his penitent not to be 'too scrupulous in setting down things, nor yet too general, but take some one or more as specimens in any kind which may have become habitual, and describe the frequency of the habit, if you can, by the number of sins in a given time, and the degree, by some aggravating circumstances, such as your conscience most reproaches you for, and He who is merciful will accept it, if fairly so intended, for a good confession.' Examination of conscience is to be done 'as a religious exercise, as in God's presence, and a good deal on your knees.'[22]

In 1846 Pusey went to Hursley to make his confession to Keble, who had reluctantly acceded to Pusey's demand that he should become his confessor. Thereafter Pusey made his confession to Keble three times a year. Pusey's correspondence with Keble, incorporated by Liddon in his *Life of Pusey*, shows Pusey using the language of the French school of Surin and Avrillon to underline the darkness of his state. 'I am scarred all over and seamed with sin, so that I am a monster to myself; I loathe myself; I can feel of myself only like one covered with leprosy from head to foot.' Pusey proposed a strict rule of life, wearing hair-cloth and using the discipline. Keble was cautious. Declaring his own lack of austerity, he implored Pusey, 'For my sake, and for all our sakes, be not hard upon yourself – remember what is said about "often infirmities".'[23]

Keble welcomed the move towards more frequent Communion, but believed it to be of the utmost importance that this should go hand in hand with a regular discipline of confession. In 1843 he wrote that 'our one great grievance is the neglect of Confession. Until we can begin to revive that, we shall not have the due severity in our religion; and without a severe religion, I fear our Church will practically fail.'[24] Coleridge, in his biography of Keble, comments that in his view Keble had both exaggerated the difficulty of ministering in a parish without a strong discipline of confession, and had failed to recognise the difficulty which would attend both on the parish priest being confessor to all his parishioners, and on the parish priest's continuing ignorance of the inner life of his flock were another priest to act as confessor even to part of the parish in his place.[25] When there were those who thought sacramental confession would never be accepted in a rural parish such as Hursley, Keble could only point to the simple folk who had clearly found spiritual comfort and relief through sacramental confession.

John Keble is perhaps most remembered for a volume of poetry, *The Christian Year*, and a sermon, the Assize Sermon of 1833 on 'National Apostasy'. The poetry will be considered later, but something must be said here about Keble as a preacher. Those who read the Assize Sermon are frequently disappointed. To be properly appreciated it must be understood in its context, as an official and public protest against a government which treated the church as but another state organisation. It was a deliberate protest on Keble's part, as we can see from a letter which has recently been given to the Keble College archive by Mrs. Margaret Allan, the great-great-granddaughter of Thomas

Keble, John's brother. John writes in this letter, dated in the earlier part of 1833, that the church in Oxford seems reluctant to take a stand, and he has accepted the vice-chancellor's invitation to preach the sermon with a view to doing just that, and he goes on to sketch the parallel he hopes to draw between his contemporary situation and to that of the Jews recalled by Samuel to their responsibilities as God's chosen people. For Newman the sermon was a prophetic sign. Newly returned from his Mediterranean journey (and near terminal illness in Sicily), the Assize Sermon was the first Newman heard on the Sunday after his return. 'I have ever considered and kept the day, the start of the religious movement of 1833' – so he wrote thirty years later in the *Apologia*.

If the Assize Sermon is more symbolically notable than theologically memorable, this is not to discount Keble as a preacher. The Oxford Movement may have been a great revival of sacramental religion, it was also a great preaching movement. First and foremost there are the eight volumes of Newman's *Parochial and Plain Sermons*, together with his *University Sermons* – of which the sermons on faith and reason and the important sermon on the development of doctrine are of outstanding theological significance the latter being in its way as creative as the later *Essay on Development*. Then there are Pusey's sermons, both moving and complex and revealing Pusey's intense mystical spirituality. They are sermons preached *coram Deo*, in the presence of God, and leading into that presence, drawing on Pusey's immense learning, not only in the Fathers but in the great tradition of spiritual writing of the Middle Ages and Counter-Reformation, as well as the seventeenth-century Anglican divines. There are ten volumes, less well known, of *Plain Sermons* by contributors to *Tracts for the Times*. A glance at the titles of these sermons gives an indication of the Tractarian theological programme and their pattern of instruction for the laity: 'Christian responsibility' – 'The certainty of judgment' – 'Our Lord a pattern of private prayer' – 'The danger of self-confidence' – 'Christian Minister, Tokens of Christ's Presence' – 'The Church Prayer Book a safe guide' – 'Holy Communion: Exceeding danger in careless receiving, death in neglecting' – 'The Transfiguration of our Lord the Earnest of the Christian's Glory' – 'Angelical Order and Obedience' – 'Christ's Baptism, a token of Pentecost'. The last two volumes, together with an additional half volume, are sermons of a somewhat different type. As the Advertisement states they 'perhaps might come more properly under the name of Catechetical Lectures. For although they have been preached as Sermons, they consist, for the most part of what had been brought forward in catechizing children after the Second Lesson.'[26] Keble was a contributor to this collection of *Plain Sermons*, though much research would be needed to identify the authors of particular sermons.

The major collection of Keble's own sermons was published posthumously (1879–1880) in eleven volumes following the sequence of the liturgical year, with additional volumes of Saints Day sermons and sermons preached on special occasions such as the consecration of Pusey's church of St. Saviour, Leeds, the fast for the Irish famine and for the Indian mutiny, anniversaries and missionary appeals. There is a further volume of *Sermons, Academical and Occasional* and another collection, edited posthumously by Pusey, of *Village Sermons on the Baptismal Service*.

In his biography of Keble, his friend Sir John Coleridge comments that Keble 'was not what is commonly called an eloquent reader or preacher; his voice was not powerful, nor his ear perfect for harmony of sound; nor had he in the popular sense great gifts of delivery; but in spite of all this, you could not but be impressed deeply both by his reading and his preaching.' 'When he preached, it was with an affectionate almost plaintive earnestness, which was very moving. His sermons were at all times full of that scriptural knowledge which was a remarkable quality in him as a divine. Like one of the old Fathers, he seemed to have caught by continual and devout study, somewhat of the idiom and manner of Scripture.'[27] Pusey, in his preface to the sermons on baptism, notes their 'affectionate simplicity'. Although in a measure appreciative of these sermons, Pusey regretted that 'through human mismanagement, it was arranged, that the writer of "the Christian Year" should, for the chief part of his life, preach to a peasant flock, of average mental capacity.' After his early university sermons and the sermon at Winchester on 'Primitive Tradition' (1836), he never preached before any intellectual audience. Late in his life the vice-chancellor of Oxford asked him to be a select preacher. Keble replied that 'his voice was no longer strong enough to be heard, and that he himself was not of the calibre for such a congregation.'[28]

In his profound study of the sermons of Bishop Lancelot Andrewes, the great seventeenth-century Anglican theologian and preacher, the Russian Orthodox theologian, Dr. Nicolas Lossky, emphasises how the sequence of Andrewes' sermons on the great festivals of the liturgical year organise the great theological themes 'into a unique vision of the mystery of salvation.' The Incarnation is central. The union of divinity and humanity in Christ 'inaugurates a new order in Creation.' In the life of the church, which is a perpetual Pentecost, the Holy Spirit sanctifies the people of God, transforming them, as Paul says, into the likeness of Christ, from one degree of glory to another. Andrewes' theology is, in the Orthodox sense of the term, 'a mystical theology.' Keble knew these sermons of Andrewes, and his own liturgical sequence of sermons serves the same purpose, though they are sermons addressed to a simpler audience and presented in a less convoluted style than his seventeenth-century predecessor.

A brief sampling of Keble's exposition of the great mysteries of the faith is all that may be permitted here. The Christmas sermons characteristically link the birth of Christ, the Son of God, with the new birth of the Christian. Keble has a great facility for evoking a sense of the wonder and mystery of the Incarnation. One of his Christmas sermons begins with these words:

> When a person wakes on a Christmas morning, and turns his mind at once, as a thoughtful person naturally will, to the great and unutterable miracle of the day, it is somewhat of the same kind of thought as when we gaze earnestly on the deep heaven above us; and the longer we gaze, the more certainly we

feel how far it reaches, how utterly and entirely beyond us; how we might go on for ever, and be more and more lost and swallowed up in the contemplation of it.[29]

As Christ's birth was hidden, humble and quiet, so the new birth of baptism. By the simplest words and actions God shares his life with us that in the end we may be partakers of his divine nature. 'Christ in the cradle, the Ancient of Days, an Infant of a few hours old, is the sure and gracious token' of God's new creation.

> 'Behold Him in that narrow manger, wrapped in those rude swaddling bands; behold Him with the eye of faith, and make thou no question, that He Who voluntarily stooped so low for thee, is able and willing to lift thee to the very highest. God made Man, God born of the Virgin, God in the swaddling bands, God in the manger, is the token and pledge of Man made Godlike, Man new-born of the Holy Ghost, Man clothed in the righteousness of God, Man exalted to the Throne of God.'[30]

The Holy Week volume includes six sets of Good Friday and Holy Week addresses: 'The Last Words of Jesus'; 'Twenty-second Psalm'; 'Old Testament types of the Cross'; 'The Lord's Prayer in Relation to the Passion'; 'Steps in the Passion'; and 'The Cross a Remedy for the Seven Deadly sins'. The Cross is the love of God stooping down to where we are. Easter is the breaking of the bonds of death and hell. Ascension is not only the Lord's return to heaven, but our being taken into the heavenly places. Pentecost is the gift of God's own life to us. Weaving in and out of Keble's explorations of the great mysteries of the faith is the sense that God's gift to us is nothing less than his own transforming life. Just as Andrewes sees Christmas, 'God with us,' completed in Pentecost, 'God in us,' − so Keble's sermons run towards the fulfillment of Ascensiontide and Pentecost. Since the Spirit 'came down at Pentecost, a new heaven and a new earth has begun here among men; all things are changed, all put in a new light, all clothed with a kind of glory from above.'[31] The common things of life God has made signs of the presence of his Spirit. 'The morning and evening dews are like His refreshing graces, ever new, never failing, given impartially to all, coming silently, but known by their purity and brightness, and by the holy hope and joy and strength, which they spread over the whole heart and life of man; not unlike the cheerful green, which follows on a timely shower in spring or summer.'[32] These can only be examples, for there is as yet no proper study of Keble's sermons.

Other aspects of Keble's ministry as parish priest and pastor must also be mentioned. He took very seriously his catechetical duties. He would take the boys and girls on alternate Sundays, and endeavour to ensure that catechizing did not become an occasion for the bright to display their ability. After the formal catechizing had finished, he would lecture from the pulpit on the subject which had been dealt with by question and answer. Children were encouraged to have their bibles in church and to follow the lessons, not just on Sundays but on weekdays. As a tutor at Oriel, a post to which he was appointed in 1817, he had brought a new conception to that office. Unless tuition was understood as a kind of pastoral care it seemed questionable to Keble for it to be appropriate for a clergyman to leave a parochial cure of souls in order to undertake it. This pastoral conception of the tutor's office was to have far-reaching consequences in providing a model for emulation by Newman and Robert Isaac Wilberforce, a model of which Provost Edward Hawkins of Oriel was to come to disapprove, when he discerned the influence Newman and his fellow tutors were having.

What Keble had practised at Oxford, he translated into a parochial context in his concern for education in the parish. He taught daily in the Boys' School from 9 a.m. until 10 a.m., and examined the pupils every Friday on what he had taught them. His curate, Peter Young, describes his teaching as simple, deep and practical, and always patient. A school inspector, later an archdeacon, came to the school and taught a class. Walking with him afterwards Keble said, 'I find that you teach children on a different principle from what I do ... you teach them analytically, and I teach them synthetically'; giving as an example the fact that the inspector had asked the children which parable taught perseverance in prayer, whereas Keble's method was to read the children the parable and ask them what lesson they learnt from it.[33] John Keble delighted in children and there are numerous testimonies to his attractiveness to them, and the simplicity and playfulness of his dealings with them, though he could equally cuff a boy for failing to show proper respect and deference to the vicar. Confirmation classes consisted of between twenty and thirty lessons, beginning with instruction on the baptism service, going on to the catechism, the confirmation service and finally the eucharist. His concern for Christian education led to his involvement with the scheme mooted by Charles Marriott for a new college in Oxford. This in the end came to nothing, but the memory of it lingered and made it seem particularly appropriate for Keble's memorial to be the Oxford college which now bears his name.

In Hursley he was assiduous in visiting the sick, or '*waiting*' on them as he liked to put it. In ministering to the dying he often used the first Good Friday collect, followed by an exhortation to the confession, the 51st Psalm, and prayers taken from the order for the Visitation of the Sick. Passages from Jeremy Taylor, Bishop Wilson and Bishop Richard Challoner were often read aloud.

Keble the parish priest; Keble the preacher; Keble the educator; Keble the spiritual guide and confessor – all of these are facets of Keble the pastor. Newman, writing of him in 1875, remembered 'what music there was in the simple earnestness and sweet gravity with which he spoke', and went on to comment that 'his keen religious instincts, his unworldly spirit, his delicacy of mind, his tenderness of others, his playfulness, his loyalty to the Holy Fathers, and his Toryism in politics, are all ethical qualities, and by their prominence give a character of their own ... to what he has written.' And Newman acknowledged that none of this could have been done without Keble's outstanding intellectual gifts.[34]

In 1850 Keble reviewed a major book on parish ministry: *Parochial Work* by Edward Monro, parish priest of Harrow Weald in Middlesex, a parish which Monro endeavoured to serve according to Tractarian principles. He was a man who believed, as John Keble himself did, that pastoral work had its own skills, discipline and method, but that beyond such things was a personal and pastoral genius which gave life and persuasive power to the methodical working of a parish. One who possessed this gift would 'go into a cottage, and with saying *very little*, not "reading the bible aloud," *doing* scarcely anything, not giving a *penny*, will come out having done a work and effected a result which other men who have not that power, with an hour's hard work at the same cottage, reading half an Epistle through, lending tracts in large print fresh from the Christian Knowledge Society, talking, arguing, reasoning, and giving half-a-crown to boot, will not effect.'[35] It was not simply a matter of professional competence, it was at heart a divine call and vocation. In his review Keble warms to Monro's sensitive advocacy of sacramental confession, approving of his Christian prudence and charity, not to say 'old English common sense' in writing and teaching about it. It was important because it was personal, and 'the foundation of all Parochial Work' was 'personal intercourse.' The daily service was likewise important and its effect was not to be measured by the number who attended. 'The fact that it is going on ... will tell upon the place, gradually and in insensible ways.'[36] Children are to be welcomed to the daily as well as the Sunday services, for instruction in church provides the important devotional context, the sense of 'religious awe', which the school-room lacks. Familiar prayers which work their way into the heart are of greater benefit that endless novelty. 'The principle of the rosary may be employed with good effect, among us as elsewhere; and especially, perhaps, in helping the devotions of the poor and unlettered. The instructing them in it may be as simple a way as any of helping them to mingle some meditation with their prayers.' And Keble goes on to suggest that the fingers may be used as a natural rosary, a trivial but eminently practical suggestion.[37] True love and sympathy, combined with plain and affectionate speech, were the consecrated gifts which communicated the gospel. Keble would have agreed with Newman's words early in his own ministry, that 'the gospel is a spirit dwelling within us and we only communicate it as we give out ourselves the while,' just as he would have approved of Newman's choice of his cardinalatial motto, *Cor ad cor loquitur*, 'heart speaks to heart' – a phrase from St. Francis de Sales, whom Newman thought Keble so closely resembled.

Keble urges the church to recruit and welcome ordinands from every section of society, but they ought not to aspire to be grand, or pompous, a scholar or a gentleman. From whatever class of society clergy came 'simplicity ... ought to be the watchword.' 'As in reading or writing, so in preaching, that course is probably best for each person which most enables him to forget himself, and to think only of God, his hearers, and his subject.'[38] The key to all is the recognition that Christianity is a supernatural life. Baptismal regeneration was so vital a doctrine to the Tractarians because it was the sacramental beginning of that supernatural life. So Keble writes: 'Admit the supernatural life of the baptized ... and all the portions of our Prayer-book, all our parochial doings will fall around it into their proper place; it is the key to the whole cypher, the screw which adjusts the whole machinery.' Such a view 'takes for granted, from beginning to end, that its subjects are all of them in a supernatural state, living among miracles, as the Jews were in the wilderness; and that all that happens to them, all they do, is proportionably ennobled and embased.'[39] Keble believes that pastoral experience has taught him that there is an implicit belief in baptismal regeneration. 'Few parents are content to be taught, or have their children taught, that infants carried out of church after Baptism, are, for aught we know, in no better spiritual condition than when they were brought in.'[40] Parochial work must be done on high sacramental principles. That Keble believes was the Prayer Book pattern, and that was his own pattern.

So glorious let Thy Pastors shine,
That by their speaking lives the world may learn
First filial duty, then divine,
That sons to parents, all to Thee may turn;
And ready prove
In fires of love,
At sight of Thee, for aye to burn.

So Keble ended his poem for St. John the Baptist's day in *The Christian Year*, expressing in poetry the pastor's calling.

Notes

1.　C.A.E. Moberly, *Dulce Domum: George Moberly* (London: T. Murray, 1911), 77–78.
2.　Charlotte M. Yonge, *Musings over the 'Christian Year' and 'Lyra Innocentium'; Together with a Few Gleanings of Recollections of the Rev. John Keble,' Gathered by Several Friends* (Oxford: J. Parker, 1871), clxv.
3.　*Ibid.*, cl–cli.
4.　*Ibid.*, cliv.
5.　Thomas Wilson, *A Short and Plain Instruction for the True Understanding of the Lord's Supper.* New Edition (London: SPCK, 1837), 102–04.
6.　J. Keble, *Letters of Spiritual Counsel and Guidance*, 3d ed., ed. R.F. Wilson (Oxford: J. Parker, 1875), xxxiii–xxxiv.
7.　*Ibid.*, xliii–xliv.
8.　*Ibid.*, 6.
9.　*Ibid.*, 8.
10.　*Ibid.*, 15.
11.　*Ibid.*, 19–23.
12.　*Ibid.*, 27.
13.　*Ibid.*, 31.
14.　J. Keble, 'Morning,' in *The Christian Year*.
15.　*Ibid.*, 45, 47.
16.　*Ibid.*, 60.
17.　*Ibid.*, 66–67.
18.　*Ibid.*, 115.
19.　*Ibid.*, 122.
20.　*Ibid.*, 204–05.
21.　*Ibid.*, 39–40.
22.　*Ibid.*, 99–100.
23.　Pusey was to give Keble a copy of Surin as a thank offering for hearing his confession; it is still preserved in Keble College library. H.P. Liddon, *Life of Edward Bouverie Pusey* (London: Longmans, Green and Co., 1894), 3:96, 109.
24.　Coleridge, 302.
25.　*Ibid.*, 313–15.
26.　*Plain Sermons*, By Contributors to the 'Tracts For The Times' (London: F. and J. Rivington, 1847), 9:1.
27.　Coleridge, 566–67.
28.　J. Keble, *Village Sermons in the Baptismal Service*, (Oxford: J. Parker, 1868), iii–iv.

29. J. Keble, *Sermons for Christmas and Epiphany* (Oxford: J. Parker, 1875), 27.
30. *Ibid.*, 63.
31. J. Keble, *Sermons for Ascension Day to Trinity Sunday* (Oxford: J. Parker, 1876), 165.
32. *Ibid.*, 169.
33. Coleridge, 569–70.
34. J. Keble, *Occasional Papers and Reviews* (Oxford: J. Parker, 1877), xiv–xvi.
35. E. Monro, *Pastoral Life* (London, 1850), pp. 36–7; quoted in Brian Heeney, *A Different Kind of Gentleman: Parish Clergy as Professional Men in Early and Mid-Victorian England* (Hamden, Connecticut: Archon, 1976), 93–4.
36. J. Keble, *Occasional Papers*, 361–62.
37. *Ibid.*, 368.
38. *Ibid.*, 370.
39. *Ibid.*, 371–72.
40. *Ibid.*, 376–77.

III The Poet

Writing of John Keble, John Henry Newman said that 'he did for the Church of England which none but a poet could do: he made it poetical.' At first sight this can seem a somewhat strange statement. If so, it is perhaps because our view of poetry is somewhat different to that of Newman and many of his contemporaries. For it is clear that Newman did not mean that Keble had made the Church of England unreal or sentimental or a matter of superifical feeling. (Not that I would wish to imply that that is our understanding of poetry.) Newman's comment underlines two important connections. First, the rediscovery by the Tractarians of the symbolic, sacramental and imaginative character of the Christian revelation. They gained this from a new appreciation of the character of Scripture, focusing not on proof texts in the manner of the older evidence theology, but on the great images and symbolic patterns of the Old and New Testaments. Hence their interest in typology. Both Pusey and Keble were Hebrew scholars: Pusey professionally as Regius professor of Hebrew; Keble in a particularly practical way with his translation of the Psalms, of which more will be said later. The more concrete and pictorial character of Hebrew thought contrasted with the abstractions of Greek theology and, even more so, with the minute propositions of scholasticism, whether in the mediaeval west, or in protestant orthodoxy. It was not for nothing that Pusey saw in the arid intellectualism of the latter one of the root causes of later rationalist scepticism in Germany. Pusey not only knew Hebrew, he also knew other Semitic languages, notably Arabic and Syriac. He was thus acquainted with the rich poetic theology of the great Syrian Father, Ephrem, and this may well have influenced his important 1836 lectures on 'Types and Prophecies'. It was characteristic of the Tractarians, as of others before them, that they saw a close connection between prophets and poets. One of John Keble's predecessors as professor of poetry at Oxford, Robert Lowth (1710–1787), who went on to be bishop successively of St. Davids, Oxford and London, published an important study, *The Sacred Poetry of the Hebrews* (1753).

These lectures, delivered like Keble's own poetry lectures in Latin, won from Keble high praise. They were, he wrote, an 'exquisite course of lectures ... which will, I trust, long secure for Latin its true place among us. We shall never feel regret for a style so finished.'[1] Leaving aside Keble's defence of lecturing in Latin, we may note Keble's appreciation of the high place Lowth gives to the poetry of the Hebrew prophets, while he is at the same time critical of what he sees as Lowth's too severe strictures on Homer. 'Surely we cannot expect from a pagan writer that he should be true to the standard of revealed religion.'[2]

Newman's comments about Keble making the Church of England poetical occur in the course of an extended review of Keble's 1846 volume of poems, *Lyra Innocentium*; a review later republished in the second volume of Newman's *Essays Critical and Historical*. In this review Newman notes how Keble, in his *Lectures on Poetry*, argued that poetry was 'a method of relieving the over-burdened mind; ... a channel through which emotion finds expression, and that a safe, regulated expression.' Poetry, in other words, has a cathartic function, providing a disciplined pattern by which the emotions may be ordered, expressed and directed. There is a parallel, which Newman draws out, between the sacramental order of the worship of the church, and raw, religious enthusiasm. So Newman writes:

> Now what is the Catholic Church, viewed in her human aspect, but a discipline of the affections and passions? What are her ordinances and practices but the regulated expression of keen, or deep, or turbid feeling, and thus a 'cleansing', as Aristotle would word it, of the sick soul? She is the poet of her children; full of music to soothe the sad and control the wayward, — wonderful in story for the imagination of the romantic; rich in symbol and imagery, so that gentle and delicate feelings, which will not bear words, may in silence intimate their presence or commune with themselves. Her very being is poetry; every psalm, every petition, every collect, every versicle, the cross, the mitre, the thurible, is a fulfillment of some dream of childhood,

or aspiration of youth. Such poets as are born under her shadow, she takes into her service; she sets them to write hymns, or to compose chants, or to embellish shrines, or to determine ceremonies, or to marshal processions; nay, she can even make schoolmen of them, as she made St. Thomas, till logic becomes poetical.[3]

As Professor Stephen Prickett comments in his book *Romanticism and Religion*, Newman senses that for Keble the 'poetic' was 'always somehow more *real* as a quality than any actual poetry.' And Newman locates the 'poetic' where he believes it belongs, in the church. 'The Catholic Church is more "poetic" than poetry itself, since poetry is only a symbol of that greater reality. She is the true catharsis.'[4]

Newman continues, with one of those powerful, ironic, contrasting passages, which he employed to such good effect in his sermons: often making use of polysyllabic, Latinate words to weigh down the position he wishes to repudiate, and using sharp and clear phrases to point up the position he wishes to affirm. Faith is not concerned with the philosophers' 'painful inductions from existing phenomena', but with the proclamation of 'Jesus and the resurrection, and "if Christ be not risen, then your faith is in vain".' So Newman represents the Anglicanism which Keble found:

all but destitute of this divine element, which is an essential property of Catholicism; – a ritual dashed upon the ground, trodden on, and broken piecemeal; – prayers, clipped, pieced, torn, shuffled about at pleasure, until the meaning of the composition perished, and offices which had been poetry were no longer even good prose; – antiphons, hymns, benedictions, invocations, shovelled away; – Scripture lessons turned into chapters; – heaviness, feebleness, unwieldiness, where the Catholic rites had had the lightness and airiness of a spirit; – vestments chucked off, lights quenched, jewels stolen, the pomp and circumstances of worship annihilated; a dreariness which could be felt, and which seemed the token of an incipient Socinianism, forcing itself upon the eye, the ear, the nostrils of the worshipper; a smell of dust and damp, not of incense; a sound of ministers preaching Catholic prayers, and parish clerks droning out Catholic canticles; the royal arms for the crucifix; huge ugly boxes of wood, sacred to preachers, frowning on the congregation in the place of the mysterious altar; and long cathedral aisles unused, railed off, like the tombs (as they were) of what had been and was not; and for orthodoxy, a frigid, unelastic, inconsistent, dull, helpless dogmatic, which could give no just account of itself, yet was intolerant of all teaching which contained a doctrine more or a doctrine less, and resented every attempt to give it meaning, – such was the religion of which this gifted author was, – not the judge and denouncer, (a deeper spirit of reverence hindered it,) – but the renovator, as far as it has been renovated.[5]

In that mammoth sentence – for it is a single sentence – Newman both implicitly praises Keble's achievement, and in a measure, reflecting his own recent move to the Church of Rome, finds it wanting. Keble's 'happy magic', he says, 'made the Anglican Church seem what Catholicism was and is. The established system found to its surprise that it had been all its life talking not prose but poetry.' Church-goers found, he went on, 'that what their pastors had spoken on, and churchwardens had used at vestry meetings, as a mere table, was "the dread altar;" and that "holy lamps were blazing;" "perfumed embers quivering bright," with "stoled priests minister at them," while the "floor was by knees of sinners worn." '[6]

Newman had no doubt that Keble's combination of poetry, devotion and personal holiness had been transforming for the Church of England. He had changed its *ethos*. And that Greek word in its modern English usage was coined by Keble. As Professor Prickett points out, 'in 1869 it was still unfamiliar enough to the general public for J.T. Coleridge to need to offer a lengthy definition of the new word.' Coleridge reminds us that the study of Aristotle was central to the Oxford of Keble's undergraduate days. Just a little later than Keble's time all undergraduates were required to pursue a detailed study of Aristotle's *Ethics, Politics, Rhetoric* and *Poetics*. In Aristotle's usage *ethos* was a moral custom or usage. Keble gave it a somewhat wider currency. So Coleridge explains: 'With Keble it imported certainly no intellectual quality, scarcely even any distinct moral one, but an habitual toning, or general colouring diffused over a man's moral qualities, giving the exercise of them a peculiar gentleness and grace.' It is to do with the way in which moral character is expressed, and so the inner reality and coherence manifested. Coleridge expounds it in the context of Keble's concern at the time of Oxford University reform that the Oxford 'ethos' should be preserved, and at the heart of that sense of the Oxford ethos was the joining of holiness and learning. Stephen Prickett comments that Keble's sense of this ideal was one which Newman made his own and developed later in his lectures on *The Idea of a University*.[7]

We can fill the word *ethos* out a little more by referring to Newman's correspondence with Blanco White (former Spanish priest and later Unitarian) in 1828. Newman speaks of the mystery of the human mind, and the personal influences that colour and shape the way we look at, grasp and understand things. 'It would be comparatively easy to enumerate the various external impulses which determine the capricious motions of a floating feather or web, and to express in an algebraical formula the line it describes' – compared with elucidating all that goes into our patterns of thought. Although we may all hold a common faith, and grasp common religious truths, we each do so uniquely, and we need to look to what we might call the underlying faith in judging the views of others. 'For *words* are not *feelings* – nor is intellect *ethos*.'[8] Newman was later on, in *The Grammar of Assent*, to develop his doctrine of the 'illative sense' partly on the basis of Aristotle's concept of *phronesis* or the intuition of moral judgement. Keble, as we see both from his manuscript commonplace book and from his treatment of the relation of faith and reason in his early university sermons, was always concerned to counter the claimed superiority of the speculative intellect by an appeal to moral sense. Intellectual gifts were talents which some had and others did not. They could therefore never be the *sine qua non* of religious faith; but

PLATE 1 *Madonna and Child*, 1943–1944,
St Matthew's Church, Northampton

PLATE 2 *Circular Altar*, St Stephen's Church, Walbrook, London EC4

PLATE 3   *Claydon Madonna and Child*, 1948, now in
St Mary's Church, Barham Suffolk

PLATE 4   *Mother and Child: Hood*, 1983, St Paul's
Cathedral, London

PLATE 5   *Two Forms*, 1934, Museum of Modern Art, New York

moral awareness was a common possession, and it was this which enlightened the mind and heart, particularly where religious truth was concerned.

> Blessed are the pure in heart,
> For they shall see our God;
> The secret of the Lord is theirs,
> Their soul is Christ's abode.

So Keble wrote in one of his poems which has become famous as a hymn. The pure in heart see God; those who live the life know the doctrine; holiness is that without which no man may see the Lord.

In 1827 Keble published *The Christian Year*. It was to become his most famous volume, selling an average of 10,000 copies a year for fifty years. Keble had published it reluctantly. It went against the grain; it offended in a sense his principle of reserve. There were those who thought that for the High Church Keble to publish such poems would mean that he would be taken for a Methodist.

The Christian Year has an important preface, or 'Advertisement', as it is called. It begins like this: 'Next to a sound rule of faith there is nothing of so much consequence as a sober standard of feeling in matters of practical religion.' The Church of England, Keble says, possesses both things in her liturgy, yet, 'in times of much leisure and unbounded curiosity, when excitement of every kind is sought after with a morbid eagerness, this part of the merit of our Liturgy is likely ... to be lost.' The 'sober standard of feeling', of the Prayer Book offices, sacraments and the round of the liturgical year, are a rich treasure, and Keble's intention in the sequence of poems which comprise *The Christian Year* is to enable this to be realised and grasped. The poems on the Occasional Services, services which are of a 'personal and domestic nature', are, Keble says, 'the most perfect instance of that *soothing* tendency in the Prayer Book,' which is his main intention in writing it.

The conjoining of feeling with creed is symptomatic of the change of sensibility that is part of the Romantic revival. Head and heart are to be conjoined, and, as Paul Tillich commented in his lectures on nineteenth century theology, emotion – the religious affections particularly – are understood to reveal truth about the human condition in a way that was not characteristic of the Enlightenment. Or, if we wished to put it in different terms, there is an attempt to reintegrate theology, so that spirituality and theology are once more conjoined; both rationalist theology and a merely experiential religion, what the eighteenth century would call 'enthusiasm', being repudiated.

Keble's reference to the '*soothing*' tendency of the Prayer Book causes us to pause. It is not an expression we would naturally use, and yet Keble clearly regards it as important. Professor Prickett points us to Keble's poem for the Fourth Sunday after Epiphany as giving us a clue. The opening stanzas portray the power of gales and storms, and the mysterious calm which follows them.

They know th'Almighty's love,
Who, when the whirlwinds rock the topmost grove,
Stand in the shade, and hear
The tumult with a deep exulting fear,
How, in their fiercest sway,
Curb'd by some power unseen, they die away,
Like a bold steed that owns his rider's arm,
Proud to be check'd and sooth'd by that o'ermastering charm.

The harnessing and directing of mighty forces, seen here in nature, is not an alien theme in Scripture. We think of the very beginning of Genesis, with the mighty wind of the Spirit sweeping over the ocean of chaos bringing order – a reminder that the Spirit is not simply untrammelled force, but ordering power. It may not be too fanciful to remember that Keble's age was the age of the industrial revolution, which although it might rape the environment could also be seen as taming and directing it – rushing streams turning mill wheels. Keble, who had been powerfully influenced by the sacramentalism of Bishop Butler's *Analogy of Religion*, which saw a pattern of type and fulfillment in nature as well as in

Scripture, goes on in his poem to draw out the parallels between the calm after storm and tempest with our inner experience.

> But there are storms within
> That heave the struggling heart with wilder din,
> And there is power and love
> The maniac's rushing frenzy to reprove;
> And when he takes his seat,
> Cloth'd and in calmness at his Saviour's feet,
>
> Is not the power as strange, the love as blest,
> As when He said, Be still, and ocean sank to rest?

Keble's poem always has a biblical reference to one of the readings for the day; in this case, the story of the demoniac whose name was legion in the episode of the Gadarene swine. The Lord's stilling of the storm was no more marvelous than the calming of the demoniac through the expulsion of the tormenting demons. We too are pointed to the same deliverer from our own inner chaos.

> And wilt thou seek again
> Thy howling waste, thy charnel-house and chain,
> And with the demons be,
> Rather than clasp thine own Deliverer's knee?
> Sure 'tis no heaven-bred awe
> That bids thee from His healing touch withdraw;
> The world and He are struggling in thy heart,
> And in they reckless mood though biddest thy Lord
>   depart.
>
> He, merciful and mild,
> As erst, beholding, loves His wayward child;
> When souls of highest birth
> Waste their impassioned might on dreams of earth,
> He opens Nature's book,
> And on His glorious Gospel bids them look,
> Till by such chords, as rule the choirs above,
> Their lawless cries are tuned to hymns of perfect love.

'Soothing' in this context is finding the 'peace of God which passes all understanding', 'the rest that remains to the people of God.' Prickett is not quite fair when he links Keble with other Victorian poets 'in search of an infantile dream world.' Prickett does, however, remind us of the older meaning of the word 'soothe': 'to prove or show to be true; to assert or uphold a truth'; or 'to give support', 'encourage', or 'confirm' – by which it reaches its weaker modern sense of 'to calm' or even 'tranquillise.'[9] The grace which Christ brings is the healing, strengthening and ordering power of the Spirit, and this is at the heart of Christian worship. Hence Keble's sense that the Prayer Book has a 'soothing tendency.'

Keble's understanding is developed in his *Lectures on Poetry*. Delivered as single lectures each term during the period when Keble held the Oxford professorship of poetry (1832–41), they were collected together and issued in their original Latin in 1844. In 1912 Edward Kershaw Francis published an English translation, assisted by Walter Lock, the warden of Keble, himself the author of a study of John Keble. The lectures are dedicated to William Wordsworth in the following terms.

TO WILLIAM WORDSWORTH
TRUE PHILOSOPHER AND INSPIRED POET
WHO BY THE SPECIAL GIFT AND CALLING OF
ALMIGHTY GOD
WHETHER HE SANG OF MAN OR OF NATURE
FAILED NOT TO LIFT UP MEN'S HEARTS TO
HOLY THINGS
NOR EVER CEASED TO CHAMPION THE CAUSE
OF THE POOR AND SIMPLE
AND SO IN PERILOUS TIMES WAS RAISED UP
TO BE A CHIEF MINISTER
NOT ONLY OF SWEETEST POETRY
BUT ALSO OF HIGH AND SACRED TRUTH
THIS TRIBUTE, SLIGHT THOUGH IT BE, IS
OFFERED
BY ONE OF THE MULTITUDE WHO FEEL EVER
INDEBTED

FOR THE IMMORTAL TREASURE OF HIS
SPLENDID POEMS
IN TESTIMONY OF RESPECT, AFFECTION AND
GRATITUDE

It was Keble's friend and biographer, J.T. Coleridge, who first introduced Keble to Wordsworth's poetry when they lived on the same staircase as fellow undergraduates at Corpus Christi College. Coleridge's uncle, the poet Samuel Taylor Coleridge, had given his nephew a copy of the *Lyrical Ballads* and the first edition of Wordsworth's *Poems*. He lent them to Keble, who read them avidly, and became a devoted admirer of Wordsworth. In 1839 Keble delivered the Creweian Oration at the university's honorary degree ceremony, in which he drew parallels between the church and the university of Oxford, saying both should be catholic, 'open to all', but Oxford, as it then was, had placed financial barriers against the poor scholars so many of its colleges were founded to support. He alluded to Wordsworth's presence in glowing terms as the one 'who of all poets, and above all has exhibited the manners, the pursuits and the feelings, religious and traditional, of the poor – I will not say in a favourable light merely, but in a light which glows with the rays of heaven.' Wordsworth's poetry would, Keble continued, be a key both to understanding and feeling 'that secret harmonious intimacy which exists between honorable Poverty ... sublime Philosophy, yea even our most holy Religion.'[10]

The overall title of Keble's lectures is *De Poeticae Vi Medica*, 'the healing power of poetry,' signalling that Keble is concerned with the spiritual purpose and character of poetry and its psychological working. On the title page Keble placed a Greek quotation from chapter seven of Plato's dialogue on poetic inspiration, *Ion*. Plato argues in this dialogue for the necessity of divine inspiration for all true poetry. You cannot be a true poet by technique alone. 'A poet is a light and winged and sacred thing, and is unable ever to indite until he has been inspired and put out of his senses.'[11] In the dialogue between Ion and Socrates, Ion describes the effect on him of reciting Homer, entering into the characters and their situation, and how the good orator enables his audience to participate in the experience he seeks to communicate, heart speaking to heart, if you like. Socrates has already explained to Ion that it is a divine force which moves him and other declaimers of poetry. It is like the force of a magnet, which can be transmitted through a series of iron rings, 'so that sometimes a long chain of iron rings is formed suspended from one another, all having the force derived from the stone. Thus the Muse herself makes people possessed and from these possessed persons there hangs a chain of others, possessed with the same enthusiasm.'[12] So the poet, the actor and the spectator are all linked together. And then comes the sentence Keble places as the motto of his lectures: 'through all these, the god draws the human mind in any direction he wishes.'[13]

Although Keble uses this text from *Ion* as the epigraph of his exposition of the nature of poetry, I would like to suggest that there are also interesting parallels with Keble's theological understanding of tradition, apostolic succession, and the principle of sacramental mediation. Keble's world is God's creation, a sacramental universe, speaking to those who read it with the eye of faith of the pattern of God's being and activity. The *locus classicus* in Keble's poetry which expresses this is perhaps the poem for Septuagesima Sunday in *The Christian Year*, one of those poems which has become part of hymnody, but a hymn now infrequently sung. The text Keble placed at the head of his poem is Romans 1.20: 'The invisible things of Him from the creation of the world are clearly seen, being understood by the things which are made.' A biblical basis for the doctrine of analogy Keble so admired in Bishop Butler is here set out. Keble opens by speaking of the book of God's creation.

> There is a book, who runs may read,
> Which heavenly truth imparts,
> And all the lore its scholars need,
> Pure eyes and Christian hearts.
>
> The works of God above, below,
> Within us and around,
> Are pages in that book, to show

How God Himself is found.

The glorious sky embracing all
Is like the Maker's love,
Wherewith, encompassed, great and small,
In peace and order move.

***

The dew of heaven is like Thy grace,
It steals in silence down;
But where it lights, the favoured place
By richest fruits is known.

***

The raging Fire, the roaring Wind,
Thy boundless power display:
But in the gentler breeze we find
The Spirit's viewless way.

Two worlds are ours: 'tis only Sin
Forbids us to descry
The mystic heaven and earth within,
Plain as the sea and sky.

Thou, who hast given me eyes to see
And love this sight so fair,
Give me a heart to find out Thee,
And read Thee everywhere.

The *Lectures on Poetry* are devoted almost entirely to a discussion of classical poetry — a reminder, as I hope my brief discussion of Keble's quotation from Plato's *Ion* has indicated, that our own for the most part non-classical education prevents us from entering fully into the implicit connections and patterns of thought of those whose minds, like Keble's, were shaped by the literary and philosophical analysis of classical texts. But although the poets discussed are Greek and Latin, Keble does spend some time discussing more general questions concerning the nature of poetry. The theme of catharsis, healing and the channelling of powerful emotions is a significant one. Poetry, Keble suggests, in his very first lecture, enables us to express and respond to overwhelming experiences. When we ponder 'on the vicissitudes of human affairs, on the marvellous ordered symmetry of the universe, or ... on the holy vision of true and divine goodness,' we can be overwhelmed. High emotion of this kind, or, at the opposite end of the scale, violent passion, is given relief by poetry. God 'has furnished amplest comfort for sufferers of either kind in the gift of Poetry.' Poetry, Keble says, is 'closely associated with measure and a definite rhythm of sound' − its structure therefore disciplines raw emotion. 'Secondly, ... its chief aim is to recall, to renew, and bring vividly before us pictures of absent objects.' It has to mark out resemblances and connections. 'In a word,' he writes, in language powerfully reminiscent of that of the poet Coleridge, 'it is the handmaid to Imagination and Fancy.' And we remember how Coleridge made this aesthetic distinction parallel to his epistemological one between reason and understanding, terms almost to be equated with faith and reason in Newman's *University Sermons*. Poetry, imposing by its discipline a proper reserve on raw emotion, has a healing character.

> Let us therefore deem the glorious art of Poetry a kind of medicine divinely bestowed upon man: which gives healing relief to secret mental emotion, yet without detriment to modest reserve: and while giving scope to enthusiasm, yet rules it with order and due control.[14]

This practical character of poetry, Keble says, has been frequently recognised. He claims originality in making it the starting point for his own explorations.

Keble's lectures are a rich vein for those concerned with literary theory, but in this context it is appropriate to focus on a few points of significance for his theology. Keble divides poets into primary poets, 'those who spontaneously moved by impulse, resort to composition for relief and solace of a burdened or over-wrought mind' − and those who are to be ranked as mere imitators, possessors of technique but not the spirit.[15] The Hebrew poetry of the prophets is amongst the most ancient, and Keble argues that in studying the prophets we find that God does not over-ride human free-will. Even when the prophets were moved by the fervour of inspiration, 'each retains his own style of speech, his individual passions, his natural character.'[16] The wisdom of God did not 'forcibly ... drive forth Nature', but gently won its way into the very heart of human nature. The human attributes and creative powers of the prophets are fulfilled, not overruled by some mechanical theory of divine dictation.

Other characteristics of primary poets are their lack of self-regard; judgement in applying a proper reserve and restraint to the imagination ('he needs but very few notes to convey his real meaning to sympathetic hearts'); and reverence for sacred things.[17] The Fathers of the church, Keble notes, practised a *disciplina arcani*, taking care to guard the Christian mysteries from opponents and mockers. 'It is with poets as with lovers and with those deeply exercised in the things of the spirit.'[18] Words need to be complemented by silence, the way of affirmation by an apophatic theology.

In his final lecture Keble turns more specifically to the relation of poetry and theology. Hebrew prophets and Greek poets were both preparations for the gospel. In them we recognise 'dispositions and tones of mind' which move beyond the things of this world. 'It was in more than one way that the Hebrew seers and poets prepared their nation to receive the later revelation of Truth. Over and above the direct teaching of their words, they indoctrinated the whole race with an undefined expectation, stimulating it to speculate about the future even by that characteristic tone of Poetry, which they ever maintain in their prophecies.'[19] The healing enabled and expressed by poetry comes close to the healing of divine grace, and it is no surprise to discover the religious character of the greatest poets. 'Poetry lends Religion her wealth of symbols and similes; Religion restores these again to Poetry, clothed with so splendid a radiance that they appear to be no longer merely symbols, but to partake (I might almost say) of the nature of sacraments.'[20] Reserve and spiritual discipline is another shared characteristic, as is the deep longing envinced in both poetry and religion for the vision of the ultimate beauty. 'Those who, from their very heart, either burst into poetry, or seek the Deity in prayer,

must needs ever cherish with their whole spirit the vision of
something more beautiful, greater and more lovable, than
all that mortal eye can see. Thus the very practice and cultivation of Poetry will be found to possess, in some sort,
the power of guiding and composing the mind to worship
and prayer.' In both poetry and religion a discipline and
effort is required. 'Be on your guard against the belief that
anything is effected by mere admiration, without effort and
action on your own part.'

> No poet will ever be great who does not constantly
> spend time and toil in studying the beauty of earth
> and sky so as to make every detail of the whole bear
> upon the object of his own love and enthusiasm: nor
> will any one make the slightest progress in holiness and
> piety who is content with the empty praises of good
> books or good men and makes no attempt to imitate
> them in his own life.[21]

For Keble, although poetry had its temptations, it was the
natural handmaid of religion. Its ordering of deep feeling was
part of the shaping of the spirit by the pattern of prayer and
liturgy. The simplest things could teach those with eyes to
see of the things of God, for as Keble wrote in that poem
for Septuagesima Sunday:

> Two worlds are ours: 'tis only Sin
> Forbids us to descry
> The mystic heaven and earth within,
> Plain as the sea and sky.

In his well-known morning hymn 'New every morning is the
love,' he takes the simple experience of waking from sleep
as a sign of the Christian's resurrection and of God's surrounding providential love. It is a theme he develops in one
of his Easter sermons.

> New every morning is the love
> Our wakening and uprising prove;
> Through sleep and darkness safely brought,

Restored to life, and power, and thought.

Keble evokes the wonder we should feel at the very simplest thing which happens to us every day when we wake from sleep. We are 'restored to life, and power, and thought.' The way of holiness is opened to us by the 'new mercies' which 'each returning day, Hover around us while we pray.' Our duty is simple: 'If on our daily course our mind, Be set to hallow all we find, New treasures still, of countless price, God will provide for sacrifice.' In verses not usually included in the version sung as a hymn. Keble speaks of those who seek to see God in all, and in all things to follow the way of self-denial.

O, could we learn that sacrifice,
What lights would all around us rise!
How would our hearts with wisdom talk
Along Life's dullest, dreariest walk!

It is indeed 'the trivial round, the common task' that provide everything needful. For Keble, like de Caussade, the present moment provides all that is needful for spiritual growth. And in the evening Keble prays that God will guide us to where it will all end:

Come near and bless us when we wake,
Ere through the world our way we take;
Till in the ocean of Thy love
We lose ourselves in Heaven above.

In the poem for the First Sunday after Christmas, Keble meditates on the powerful emotions arising in the heart when we desperately desire to undo what has happened, to go back to where we were before this or that sin and failure. We long for a miracle like that recorded in Isaiah 38.8, when, in answer to King Hezekiah's prayer, the sun went backward ten degrees. Keble knows how good Christians fail, and the keen faith of those who vow themselves to God's service is dulled by the passing of time and the world's corruption.

Bright hopes, that erst the bosom warmed,
And vows, too pure to be performed,
And prayers blown wide by gales of care:
These, and such half-waking dreams,
Like stormy lights on mountain streams,
Wavering and broken all, athwart the conscience glare.

How, Keble asks, 'shall we 'escape th' o'erwhelming Past?'
It is by love alone that we can be changed, a love which
transforms our tears.

We would not have them stain'd and dim,
But dropp'd from wings of Seraphim,
All glowing with the light accepted Love imparts.

Time's waters will not ebb nor stay,
Power cannot change them, but Love may;
What cannot be, Love counts it done.
Deep in the heart, her searching view
Can read where Faith is fixed and true,
Through shades of setting life can see Heaven's work
  begun.

O Thou, who keep'st the Key of Love,
Open Thy fount, eternal Dove,
And overflow this heart of mine,
Enlarging as it fills with Thee,
Till in one blaze of charity
Care and remorse are lost, like motes in light divine;

Till, as each moment wafts us higher,
By every gush of pure desire,
And high-breath'd hope of joys above,
By every sacred sigh we heave,
Whole years of folly we outlive,
In His unerring sight, who measures Life by love.

Keble knew that the work of grace was silent and mysterious.
Like the dew of heaven 'it steals in silence down.' Faith and
holiness may shine with a splendour and brilliance but yet
remain hidden, dwelling 'unseen by all but Heaven, Like
diamond blazing in the mine.'

Keble was a practitioner of what he preached and wrote. The editor of his *Miscellaneous Poems* (1869) observed that it was the characteristic of Keble's poetry 'to be in a very high degree the reflex of himself.' He suggested that, except for the ode he composed for Wordsworth's honorary degree, that Keble had never sat down with the express purpose of writing poetry, 'but gifted with a mind highly poetical by nature, and refined by the highest cultivation, it was a relief to him, as various circumstances arose, to express in verse the thoughts and feelings which those circumstances suggested.'[22] Very slight incidents, a child's question, or some aspect of nature, might spark a poem, which might be written on the back of a letter, or on the leaf of an old pocket book. His encomium on Wordsworth for being the poet of the poor was recognised by Keble in his educational concerns, whether in the village school at Hursley or in his desire to see Oxford returning to its original foundation for poor scholars, thus becoming truly catholic once more. Isaac Williams, another Tractarian poet-priest, whose life was changed by his participation in Keble's reading parties at Southrop, noted Keble's very different attitude to the poor from that which he had encountered at Harrow, his public school. There, he recorded, 'the poor were never spoken of but by some contemptuous term – looked upon as hateful boors to be fought with, or cajoled for political objects; but for them to be looked upon with tender regard and friendship, more than the rich, and in some cases even referred to as instructors of that widsom which God teaches them, this was a new world to me.'[23]

One further contribution of Keble the poet must be touched on before I conclude. It is not generally known that in 1839 Keble published a metrical translation of the Psalms. The first edition of a thousand copies was exhausted within the month. The project was one dear to Keble's heart at a time when hymns were still rarely sung in Anglican services, and metrical psalms were almost the only congregational music available. Keble considered that the older metrical versions were often banal as poetry and unfaithful to the original Hebrew. Pusey, as a Hebraist, encouraged Keble in his project, and vetted the translation in minute detail between

1836 and 1838. There was some hope on publication that Bishop Richard Bagot of Oxford, to whom the psalter is dedicated, might have been persuaded to licence it for liturgical use in the diocese. In the end, as the dedication wording recognised, it simply appeared under Bagot's sanction.'[24]

In the preface Keble comments that his fidelity to the original Hebrew may have resulted for some in disappointment that 'the mystical and evangelical meaning of the Psalms is not so much brought out as it might have been.' Keble is unrepentant. His approach is, he believes, consonant with God's general pattern of revelation. That is, 'to disclose, rather than exhibit His dealings and His will; to keep Himself, to the generality, under a veil of reserve, through which the eyes of men might see just so much and so clearly, as they were purged by Faith and Purity and Obedience.' Again there is the stress on only the pure of heart seeing God, as well as a reflection of Keble's understanding of poetry. 'Considering the Psalms especially as divine *Poems*, this surely is a quality which we should expect to find in them: a certain combination of reserve with openness being of the very essence of poetry: and the Psalms being apparently ordained to leaven the poetry of the whole world, as the history of the Old Testament to be 'the Sun of all other histories".'[25] Although the church had always used the Psalms with reference to Christ, to the church and to the individual Christian the translator ought not to impose a single meaning, where the ambiguity is important for conveying the meaning. The full resonance of language needs to be preserved, and the Christian theologian is committed, in F.D. Maurice's words, 'to as simple a statement of the case, as the case itself permits.' Of all the Tractarians perhaps it was Newman who was most aware that doctrinal definition can be both a creative crystallisation and also a narrowing. There is widsom in the church having been a reluctant definer. 'Reserve', which might be described in part as a proper reverence and humility before the mystery of God, is to be practised not only in the way Christian truth is proclaimed (a religion of the heart need not be worn upon the sleeve), but also in the way it is expressed. 'Doctrine lying hid in language' may mean that poetry with its images and symbols may be a more appropriate medium of expression than formal statement, and it is certainly of a piece with the common conviction of all the Tractarians that prayer, worship, the quest for holiness and theological reflection belong inseparably together.

Keble's metrical version of the Psalms still repays study. As J.T. Coleridge noted, Keble's psalms did not become part of the worshipping life of the church for they were overtaken by the more general adoption of hymns in Anglican worship, though it is perhaps surprising that some of his psalms did not find a place in hymn books. If so, it may be because of his overriding concern for accuracy in translation, sometimes at the expense of felicitous phraseology.[26] But that cannot be a universal judgement, and there are many instances where the words are powerful to convey the meaning. The other reason for the failure to become widely used is one which Keble notes in his own preface. The Psalms were, he says, originally designed for chanting, not singing; but the Anglican custom in which he had been brought up, and which was almost universal, was to sing metrical versions. Keble thought that the chanting of psalms was a lost battle. He was wrong, and it was the influence of the Oxford Movement that was largely responsible.

Having spoken of Keble's psalter, let me now give a few examples of his work. Psalm 23, for instance, begins with the following two stanzas.

> My Shepherd is the Lord; I know
> No care, nor craving need:
> He lays me where the green herbs grow
> Along the quiet mead:
>
> He leads me where the waters glide,
> The waters soft and still,
> And homeward He will gently guide
> My wandering heart and will.

The 'care and craving need' capture well the sense of consuming, fretful anxiety from which God's providential care promises us deliverance.

Then there is Psalm 22, the great psalm of the Passion.

> Thou from the womb didst set me free:
> When on my mother's breasts I hung,
> My trusting heart was all of Thee,
> A foundling in Thy kind arms flung;
>
> Flung from the birth, to live or die;
> My God from mine own mother's womb!
> O go not far, for grief is nigh,
> And none at hand to stay my doom.

The repetition of the powerful word 'flung' at the end of one verse and the beginning of the next in two totally contrasting contexts — flung into the embracing arms of God, and flung from the womb, and yet for all the pain and suffering, flung in the end nowhere else but into the arms of God — is indeed compelling. Or there is Psalm 139.

> Lord, Thou hast search'd me out, and known
> My rising up and lying down;
> Thou knowest them all; each thought in me
> Far off is deeply traced by Thee.
>
> ***
>
> Then said I, 'Darkness sure will hide;'
> But night was day on every side:
> The darkness is not dark with Thee,
> By day and night, Thy beams are free.
>
> Gloom is as light, and light as gloom;
> My reins and heart are Thine,
> Thy work, Thy purchase: in the womb
> I felt the wing divine.
>
> I thank Thee, for in fearfulness
> And wonder I am wrought:
> Thy works, how dread, my soul oppress
> With ever-deepening thought.
>
> My very self, that hidden spark,

Was known to Thee ere birth.
Though framed and fashioned in the dark,
Here in the low, cold earth!

Thine eyes beheld me as I lay,
Eere face or form began,
And in Thy book from day to day
Was marked the growing man.

Keble was keenly aware of the inner dynamics of the spiritual life. We have seen this in his work as a pastor; it is no less present in his understanding of how poetry can enable spiritual growth, 'soothing' (in the old sense of that word) our inner hurts and pains. The love of God sets us free, but does so in a way which respects our freedom. Keble believes firmly and truly, but also deeply. His pastoral work taught him that the humble poor know more of the mystery of God than the rich and powerful, whether in material possessions or in intellect. He would have shrunk from the church bureaucracies, the committees and procedures of our day. He exalted the high calling of every Christian, a high understanding of God's grace in word and sacraments, a high and holy understanding of ministry — but he was aware of the temptations of power and the deceits of flattery. It was his humility which impressed, a humility grounded in love.

Some years ago Father Hugo Rahner, the brother of the more famous Karl, a fellow-Jesuit and also a brilliant intellect, wrote a little book of which the English title is *Man at Play: or, did you ever practise eutrapelia?* Eutrapelia is a virtue extolled by Aristotle in his *Ethics*, where Keble would have certainly read about it. Eutrapelia is the virtue of those who know how to play aright, 'they are able to turn aptly into laughter what is said or done.' The Greek *aner-spoudogeleios* — the 'grave-merry man' — becomes in Clement of Alexandria the one who sees life in an important aspect as a 'divine children's game.' 'The game of grace', known by those who have a child-like humility is, Rahner says, the profound life of the church, where the one who is truly Catholic 'answers the game of grace with his counter-play of liturgy and sacrament, so that Church, grace and liturgical action becomes for him no more than a prelude to that final carefree gaiety of heart, which he will experience one day in the everlasting game of the Beatific Vision.'[27] Keble, I believe, had that virtue in abundance, and it was part of his attractiveness. He loved children and their ways, even though he and his wife were childless. His volume of poems, *Lyra Innocentium*, centres on the windows into eternity provided by the minute particulars of children's lives and words. Isaac Williams recorded Keble's rustic gardener and groom at Southrop as saying, 'Master is the greatest boy of the lot.' And Williams himself wrote of how overcome he had been in finding that Keble, the renowned Oxford double-first, 'the wisest of the wise, and the most learned of men', was 'more full of playful jest than a boy, so full of love and good nature.' 'In his intercourse with us ... there was such an absence of all authority or preaching of religion that it might have been asked where all this transforming power was, when there appeared nothing but affectionate playfulness.'[28]

St. Gregory of Nyssa, commenting on the Septuagint version of Psalm 52, writes of the superscription 'Unto the end, for Maeleth', that it is about the end of time and 'Maeleth' means 'for the dancing chorus.' It speaks, therefore, of the blessed dance that will be ours at the end of days. Original sin has destroyed the dance-like harmony of the spirit. Only 'in the end' will all be restored, and humanity will once again take part in the dancing chorus. Do not succumb, says Gregory, 'in the battle against temptation ... but look steadfastly forward to the final victory. And this victory will come and thou shalt be found in the dancing ranks of the angelic spirits.'[29] All is by grace, for the saints are, as Keble himself put it, 'the Saviour in His people crowned.' That crown of dancing grace was assuredly at the heart and the end of the life of the servant and priest of God, John Keble, for whom we give thanks and praise.

So glorious let Thy Pastors shine,
That by their speaking lives the world may learn
First filial duty, then divine,

That sons to parents, all to Thee may turn;
And ready prove
In fires of love,
At sight of Thee, for aye to burn.

***

Notes

1. J.Keble, *Lectures on Poetry, 1832–1841*, trans. E.K. Francis (Oxford: Clarendon, 1912), 1:16.
2. *Ibid.*, 182.
3. J.H. Newman, *Essays Critical and Historical*, 3rd ed. (London: B.M. Pickering, 1873), 2:442–3.
4. Stephen Prickett, *Romanticism and Religion: The Tradition of Coleridge and Wordsworth in the Victorian Church* (Cambridge: University Press, 1976), 119.
5. Newman, *Essays*, 2:443–44.
6. *Ibid.*, 444–45.
7. Coleridge, *A Memoir of the Rev. John Keble*, 398; Prickett, 96–97.
8. J.H. Newman to J.B. White, March 1, 1828, in *The Letters and Diaries of John Henry Newman*, ed. Ian Ker and Thomas Gornall (Oxford: Clarendon Press, 1979), 2:59–60.
9. Prickett, 112–13.
10. Coleridge, 260.
11. Plato, *Ion*. 533E.
12. Plato, *Ion*, 533, *Ancient Literary Criticism*, ed. D.A. Russell and M. Winterbottom (Oxford: Clarendon Press, 1972), 43.
13. Plato, *Ion*, 536, *Ibid.*, 44.
14. J. Keble, *Lectures on Poetry*, 1:22.
15. *Ibid.*, 53.
16. *Ibid.*, 61.
17. *Ibid.*, 73.
18. *Ibid.*, 75–76.
19. *Lectures*, 2:474–75.
20. Ibid., 481.
21. *Ibid.*, 482–83.
22. J. Keble, *Miscellaneous Poems* (New York: Pott & Amery, 1869), xvi. The editor was George Moberly.
23. Isaac Williams, *Autobiography*, 2nd ed., ed. George Prevost (London: Longmans, Green & Co., 1892), 20.
24. H.P. Liddon, *Life of E.B. Pusey* (London: Longmans, Green, & Co., 1893), 2:113–17.

25. J. Keble, *The Psalter or Psalms of David in English Verse*, 3rd ed. (1840), xi.
26. Coleridge, *Memoir*, 257–58.
27. Hugo Rahner, *Man At Play*, trans. B. Battershaw and E. Quinn (London: Burns & Oates, 1965), 10.
28. Williams, 18, 20, 27.
29. Gregory of Nyssa, 'Homiliae in Psalmos, 6;' quoted in Rahner, 89–90.

The Priest in Anglicanism

Part I: Priestly Lives and Ministries

1) John Keble

The editor of the first American edition of John Keble's *The Christian Year*, George Washington Doane, second bishop of New Jersey, in his introduction to that volume published in 1834, remarked that 'The author of these pieces, ... while he holds the most honourable office of Professor of Poetry in the University of Oxford, is [also] the exemplary and faithful pastor of a humble country congregation, and devotes himself unsparingly to the spiritual welfare of a rustic flock, in which there is scarcely a single family of rank or education.'[1] Parish priest of Hursley for thirty years from 1836 to his death in 1866, and for part of the same time professor of poetry at Oxford, 1831 to 1841 (it is said that his duty in the chair at Oxford only required him to give one lecture a year!), Keble is the one whom we remember as 'Priest, Pastor, and Poet' (his tag for March 29 in the *Alternative Service Book* of the Church of England).[2]

In this essay on 'The Priest in Anglicanism,' I want to begin by underlining, as the second bishop of New Jersey's remarks intimated in 1834, that Keble's own legacy of priesthood to Anglicanism consists both of a particular priestly life lived – his own – as well as of a doctrine of priesthood sketched in poetical and theological writing that is part of the greater and more general Anglican doctrinal tradition. Earlier in this series an introduction to the legacy of priesthood from Keble to us today has already been given, and I only wish in this first part of my essay to offer some few additional remarks and citations that relate to his teaching on this subject before I turn to my broader assignment of 'The Priest in Anglicanism.'

First, and in its own way more profound on the subject than any of the poems of *The Christian Year*, are Keble's lines from the *Lyra Innocentium*, 'The Songs of the Innocents,' published in January of 1843. Here we perceive his doctrine of priesthood in his own words. There is a sacramental profundity that still speaks to us today:

A mortal youth I saw
Nigh to God's Altar draw
And lowly kneel, while o'er him pastoral hands
Were spread with many a prayer,
And when he rose up there,
He could undo or bind the dread celestial bands.

When bread and wine he takes,
And of Christ's Passion makes
Memorial high before the mercy throne,
Faith speaks, and we are sure
That offering good and pure
Is more than angels' bread to all whom Christ will own.

'Mid mourners I have stood,
And with sad eye pursued
The coffin sinking in the grave's dark shade:
The immortal life, we know,
Dwells there with hidden glow,
Brightly to burn one day when sun and stars shall fade.

What is this silent might,
Making our darkness light,
New wine our waters, heavenly blood our wine?
Christ with His mother dear,
And all His saints, is here,
And where they dwell is heaven, and what they touch,
    divine.'[3]

We commemorate in this symposium the 200th anniversary of Keble's birth, 1792 to 1992, and not his famous Assize Sermon, preached in 1833 and later regarded by Newman and some others as the beginning of the Oxford Movement, nor his essentially conservative ideology and his total opposition to the so-called 'liberalism' of his own day.

There is nonetheless one other piece of Keble's theology of priesthood, a very specific doctrinal teaching, that I want to call to our attention in these introductory remarks, and this is his emphasis upon the absolute necessity of episcopal ordination in the historic succession for the conferral of the sacred priesthood. This is, as he put it in the preface to his edition of the works of Richard Hooker (published in 1841): 'the necessity, namely, of the apostolical commission to the derivation of sacramental grace, and to our mystical communion with Christ.'[4] Keble makes this point in the context of observing that Hooker had allowed conditions such as 'extreme necessity,' 'the impossibility of procuring a bishop to ordain,' and 'supernatural calling' as grounds for waiving the requirement of episcopal ordination. He notes that Hooker's position, though, represents something of a development in a catholic direction, since 'nearly up to the time when [Hooker] wrote, numbers had been admitted to the ministry of the Church of England, with no better than Presbyterian ordination'! And then, continuing his acknowledgement of this historical trajectory, Keble discerns what he calls 'a marked distinction' between the era of Hooker, when such exceptions were tolerated, and that of 'the two next generations,' when they were not. Both eras 'regarded the order of Bishops as being immediately and properly of Divine right,' Keble says; but he adds that the next generation of divines after Hooker entered on this subject 'fresh from the discovery of the remains of St. Ignatius' of Antioch, and this, he concludes, made all the difference to those who followed after Hooker. The genuine epistles of St. Ignatius of Antioch, discovered and identified only in the seventeenth century, as Keble remarks at more than one place in his introduction to Hooker's works, portray the episcopate as a separate and even higher order than the priesthood. Here he is perhaps reflecting the influence of Henry Hammond and he is certainly developing a doctrine of apostolic succession, based on Ignatius and the Book of Acts, that he had already anticipated in *Tract* 52, which he published in 1835.

Hence Keble concludes that the Anglican doctrine of priesthood in the era following Hooker took properly a

higher and stricter view of the necessity of episcopal ordination for the conferral of sacramental priesthood because
it was willing to yield to the facts of historical discovery
regarding 'the frame[work] of the visible Church.' Keble
does not condemn Hooker for allowing such exceptions
to episcopal ordination, Keble admits the historical development of doctrine, Keble believes that such historical
research can cause the church to alter and even tighten
its visible framework, and all this he implies in the midst
of affirming the necessity of episcopal ordination itself, in
the historic succession, for the conferral of sacramental
priesthood. How brilliant, how profoundly catholic, one
may observe!

All this can be found in Keble's contribution to the
Anglican doctrine of priesthood, just as his ministry itself,
especially his thirty years as a priest at Hursley, was his contribution to the priestly life. But the subject of my essay is
broader.

2) Anglicanism

As I turn from Keble's particular contribution to the more
general topic of 'The Priest in Anglicanism,' I want to begin
by rejecting the view that would date the beginnings of
Anglicanism only with the Protestant Reformation of the
sixteenth century or the view that would speak of so-called
'classical' Anglicanism and then date it only from the seventeenth century. Such views would indeed make my present
task much easier, for I would not have to begin with the
earliest evidence of priesthood in England, or indeed with
any evidence at all before the sixteenth or seventeenth centuries, but I respectfully believe such views are wrong, on
theological and linguistic grounds as well as on historical
ones. It is impossible to claim, as we Anglicans do, that
our church, and indeed our priesthood, *since* the Reformation is continuous in doctrinal essentials with that which
went *before* the Reformation, if one dates the beginnings
of Anglicanism merely from the sixteenth or seventeenth
centuries. Likewise, it is impossible to claim that 'Anglicanism' – that word – stands for some one, and only

one, set of clearly defined doctrinal beliefs, usually corresponding rather closely with the particular prejudices of the person who is defining it, when in fact the term 'Anglicanism' itself originates in recorded speech, according to the latest *Oxford English Dictionary*, only from the year 1838.[5] To claim that the concept existed before the term was being used, is to define the term subjectively and anachronously. The term originated in fact with Newman, using it not in a doctrinal sense but in a geographical one, the sense in which I would use it, namely as 'the church tradition, life, *and* doctrine present in and coming from England ("Angle-land") since the earliest existence of Christianity in that land.' This describes our church, and the changes of the Reformation were only secondary, not essential. This therefore will be my working definition of Anglicanism in this essay, and this definition enables and obligates me to identify and discuss now the very first instance of 'The Priest in Anglicanism,' which is my subject.

3) The Priest who Converted Alban

So it is that I take Anglicanism historically to originate *not* from 1838, the earliest recorded use of the term, *nor* from the sixteenth or seventeenth centuries, a limitation of origin so dear to protestant minds (especially to those who do not specialize in the Latin sources prior to these centuries), but rather to date from the earliest recorded traces of Christianity in England. I take it back to the patristic period of the late second century when the Christian faith first arrived there, back to the first martyr of that land, St. Alban, in the early third century, and back to the first recorded evidence of a priest in that land, the priest whom later tradition has, probably erroneously, named 'Amphibalus.'[6] It was that priest, whatever his name was and we don't really know, who according to tradition converted Alban while Alban was sheltering him from persecution, whose cloak was then worn by Alban when he was martyred. It is that priest who is the prime candidate to be the very first priest in Anglicanism about whom anything is known. This is certainly so if 'Anglicanism' is understood geographically as pertaining to Christianity in or from England rather than doctrinally as restricted to one particular belief held tenaciously by later protestant Reformers. The first priest in Anglicanism, then, was this priest later erroneously given the name Amphibalus (after the cloak he lent to Alban), who converted Alban to Christianity and in whose place Alban himself is said to have been martyred, consequent to his conversion, probably in the early third century. Unless one attempts to limit Anglicanism doctrinally to something much later and to something much less than the total catholic Christian faith as it has waxed and waned and waxed and waned over centuries of history in England, unless one imposes such limitations, then we must say that the earliest priest in Anglicanism about whom we know anything is the one whom Alban sheltered. And it is interesting to note, in this decade of evangelism being observed throughout the Anglican Communion, that the principal recorded activity of that first priest in Anglicanism was conversion. He, by the grace of God, was God's human instrument for the conversion of Alban to Christianity, as later Christian historians have come to see him. Indeed, Alban's conversion was so thorough that Alban was immediately willing to die for that faith, as die he did and that forthwith. It is indeed noteworthy that the principal recorded activity of the first priest in Anglicanism was, as we would say today, proclamation and evangelism. 'Gradually instructed by this priest's teaching of salvation,' the Venerable Bede tells us, 'Alban renounced the darkness of idolatry, and sincerely accepted Christ.'[7] Humanly speaking, we have that priest to thank, whatever his name, for the witness and even blood-martyrdom of the proto-martyr of England, St. Alban.

Now if I have identified the person and told the story of this first priest in Anglicanism in some detail here, it is of course obvious that I can not do the same for every subsequent Anglican priest. There are thousands and thousands of priests in Anglicanism about whom many stories could be told, some edifying and some not, and it will be my contention in the final section of this essay that, underneath all this diversity of priestly lives and writings, there is a central consistency of doctrine about priesthood in Anglicanism, to which Keble's doctrine that I have already explained also bears witness. Thus I will summarize and anticipate my conclusion: to survey 'The Priest in Anglicanism' is to reveal a rich plurality and diversity of priestly lives and ministries but also a central consistency of doctrine about priesthood that is consonant with the main line of catholic teaching that goes back even to the patristic period when it was being shaped and when the land we now call England was giving birth to what would, after 1838, be called 'Anglicanism.'

'The Priest in Anglicanism,' then, is not a tidy subject, and I believe it is to our credit that Anglicans have been willing to recognize this fact and even to laugh at it. For example, I have long been fascinated by a book of 291 pages published in the year 1855 and entitled, *The Absence of Precision in the Formularies of the Church of England; Scriptural, and Suitable to a State of Probation!*[8]

Now I turn, only for the purpose of illustration and not for completeness or even comprehensiveness, to a rather minimal and highly selective survey of the lives, ministries, and writings on priesthood that constitute the legacy of some of the priests in Anglicanism over the course of history. We have considered Keble and the so-called Amphibalus, and we shall look at eight others for a total of ten, in a catena of citations and passages intended to let these priests speak in their own words. It is intended merely to be evocative but by no means exhaustive or even fully representative, and it is intended only as a prelude to my consideration of the doctrine of priesthood in Anglicanism, which will be the final section of this essay.

4) The Venerable Bede

Next after the priest who converted St. Alban, I want to note the Venerable Bede, 'the servant of Christ and priest of the monastery' [of Jarrow, near Durham], as he calls himself, whose dates are 672–735. 'I was born on the lands of this monastery,' he tells us, 'and on reaching seven years of age I was entrusted by my family first to the most reverend Abbot Benedict and later to Abbot Ceolfrid for my education. I have spent all the remainder of my life in this monastery and devoted myself entirely to the study of the Scriptures. And while I have observed the regular discipline and sung the choir offices daily in church, my chief delight has always been in study, teaching, and writing.'[9] Bede's *Ecclesiastical History* is still the principal source for the early history of England, and he was, as his biographer in *Lesser Feasts and Fasts* tells us, 'an exemplary monk, an ardent Christian, devoted scholar, and a man of pure and winsome manners.'[10] He is, thus, an outstanding early model of 'the priest in Anglicanism.'

5) St. Aelfric of Eynsham

I turn to two other sources of priesthood for this early period, of which the first is the pastoral letters of St. Aelfric of Eynsham, written in the late tenth century. Here we find some codification of the standards for priestly life, standards that would largely become the priestly norm for the English Middle Ages, some familiar standards that we can recognize and yet others that surprise us in their dissimilarity to what we would expect. Let us consider some of the admonitions for priests contained within the pastoral letter written by Aelfric for Wulfsige III, Bishop of Sherborne from 993 to 1001:

> Christ himself established Christianity and chastity, and all those who journeyed in his company abandoned all worldly things and the society of women ... Neither bishop nor mass-priest, nor deacon, nor any regular canon, is to have in his house any woman, unless it be his mother or his sister, his father's sister or his mother's sister, and he who does otherwise is to forfeit his orders. Now this seems to you strange to hear, because you have made your wretched behaviour so customary, as if there were no harm in a priest living just like a married man. Now you say that you cannot live without the services of a woman. But how could the holy men then live without a wife? ...
> Presbiter is the mass-priest or elder. Not that each is old, but that he is old in wisdom. He consecrates

God's eucharist, just as the Saviour commanded. He shall teach the people in the faith with preaching and set an example to Christians with pure conduct. And his life shall not be like that of laymen. There is no further difference between a mass-priest and a bishop except that a bishop is appointed to ordain priests and to confirm children and to consecrate churches and to watch over God's dues, for it would be too manifold if every mass-priest did so; and they have one and the same order, although the second stands higher ... These orders are holy and bring to heaven the souls of those priests who observe them cleanly.

Now it befits mass-priests and all God's servants that they maintain their churches with holy service, and sing the seven canonical hours therein which are appointed for them ... And they are to pray zealously for the king and for their bishop and for those who do good to them, and for all Christian people. [The mass-priest] shall have also the weapons for that spiritual work, before he is ordained, namely, the holy books: a psalter and a book with the epistles, an evangeliary and a missal, songbooks and a manual, a computus and a passional, a penitential and a reading-book. These books the priest must needs have, and he cannot be without them, if he wishes to observe his order rightly and to direct correctly the people who belong to him ... And he must also have mass-vestments, so that he can serve God himself honourably, as is fitting, and his vestments are not to be dirty nor, indeed, worn out; and his altar cloths are to be in good condition. His chalice also is to be made of clean material, imperishable, and also the paten; and (he is to have) a clean corporal, as befits Christ's services ...

The mass-priest shall tell to the people on Sundays and festivals the meaning of the gospel in English; and about the paternoster and about the creed also, as often as he can, as an incitement to men, that they may know the faith and observe their Christianity ...

And if an unbaptized child is brought suddenly to the mass-priest, he must baptize it immediately in haste, so that it does not die heathen. And no priest is to do his holy service for money, nor ask anything for it, neither for baptism nor for any service ... Now the servant of God is not to do God's service for money, but to the end that he may merit the eternal glory through it. Nor is any priest out of any covetousness to move from one church to another, but ever to remain in that to which he was consecrated, as long as his life lasts. Nor is any priest through foolishness to drink immoderately, nor to compel any man to much drinking, because he must be ready, so that he has his wits, if a child is to be baptized or a man to be given the sacrament. And even if it does not happen so, he must not be drunk, because our Lord forbade drunkenness to his servants. Nor is a priest to be a trader or covetous merchant; nor is he to desert his religious vocation, nor to take part in secular suits; nor is he to bear weapons, nor to start strife; nor is he to drink at the wine-casks, as laymen do; nor is he to swear oaths, but ever speak truthfully with simplicity, as a learned servant of God. He must also impose penance on sinners with discretion, each according to his measure, as each can support. And he must give the sacrament to the infirm and the sick, while the sick man can swallow the sacrament; and he must not do it if he is only half-alive, for Christ commanded that the sacrament should be eaten. The priest must have consecrated oil separately for children and separately for sick men, and always anoint the sick in their illness ... You shall not be glad about men's decease, nor attend on the corpse unless you are invited to it. When you are invited to it, you are then to forbid the heathen songs of the laymen and their loud laughter. Nor are you yourselves to eat or drink in the place where the corpse lies, lest you are imitators of the heathenism which they practice there.

Nor shall you be proud, adorned with rings; nor shall your clothing be made too showily, nor again too meanly; but each is to be dressed as befits his order, so that the priest have that to which he is consecrated. And he is not to wear a monk's garb or that of a layman any more than the man wears women's apparel.

Christ spoke concerning his servants who serve him eagerly that they should be ever in bliss with him, where he himself is in the true life, to whom is glory and honour ever into eternity. Amen.[11]

6) Wulfstan

Another picture of the priest in Anglicanism comes from the writings associated with the great archbishop of York in the early eleventh century, Wulfstan, a distinguished author, conscientious prelate, and ecclesiastical reformer of the late Anglo-Saxon church. First, I cite from what are probably the earliest surviving Anglican 'Examination Standards for Candidates for Ordination,' which date from this time and are associated with his name:

Those are worthy of honour before God and also before the world who attain the high order by right and afterwards keep it rightly. But it is a great pity that there are too many who desire the high order more than they should; and namely those especially who can least understand what they should most understand in that order. Now we wish henceforth to be to some extent more cautious about that than we have been hitherto. He who desires orders is to come to the bishop one month before the time of ordination, and be then under examination where the bishop directs; and he is to take heed that he has for that period the sustenance in food and fodder which he should have, so that he is not at all a burden for those things on him who has to examine him ...

First, then, this is the beginning of the examination: of what faith he is and how he can explain the true faith to other men, and what he clearly understands about what has come to pass through God or is still to come to pass. Next, how he knows his ministry, and how he understands baptism, and how he comprehends the symbolism of the mass and also of the other church services; and whether he knows the canons to any extent; next, how he can divide the course of the year by computation. If he is certain in all these things, he is then the better worthy [wyrde] of orders. If he then knows too little of these things, he is first to learn, and afterwards receive orders. And nevertheless, if one must for necessity ordain a half-educated man, who knows all too little, one is then to do so, if there is great necessity, on condition that he find surety for himself that he will learn afterwards as eagerly as ever he possibly can.

When it is the time of ordination, and those whom he shall ordain are brought to the bishop, he will then wish to know to what he is to ordain them, and from whose hand he is to receive them, and who is to receive them back at his hands according to the conditions which they then make; that is, that he (the teacher) who recommends him to him (the bishop), is to know how worthy he is of orders and how he has previously conducted himself towards God and towards men. He is to give the truest account of what he knows about him, and then deliver him into the bishop's hand, and after he has been ordained, receive him back, and he is to pay heed afterwards how he henceforward observes his orders. If he violates anything, and he knows it about him, he is to compel him, if he can, to make amends, or he will be responsible along with him at God's judgement, if he is not willing to admonish him previously for his advantage.

And he who receives the high orders, if he is a mass-priest, is to celebrate thirty masses for his bishop, and a deacon is to sing thirty psalters, and in addition they are ever to pray zealously for him for their whole lifetime.[12]

7) Law of the Northumbrian Priests

Next I cite from the so-called *Law of the Northumbrian Priests*, a set of regulations for the priests of the diocese of York which has been dated to *c.* 1008 – 1023 and is also associated with the name of Archbishop Wulfstan:

If anyone offer wrong to any priest, all his colleagues are to be zealous about obtaining the compensation with the help of the bishop ... And by virtue of God's prohibition we forbid that any priest shall either buy or receive another's church, unless anyone commits a capital crime so that he is not henceforth worthy to minister at the altar. And if any priest does so in other circumstances, he is to forfeit his dignity and the friendship of his colleagues, and he is not to celebrate mass anywhere until he who rightly owns the church is in possession of it.

And each priest is to provide himself with twelve sureties, that he will rightly observe the priests' law. And if any priest commits an offence, and he celebrates mass in spite of the bishop's prohibition, he is to pay twenty ores for disregard of the prohibition, and in addition make amends for the offence which he previously committed.

There then follows a long series of prohibitions, of things that a priest may not do, each of which is followed by a corresponding penalty and a requirement to make amends. I give here the prohibitions, but not the penalties that follow each of them:

If a priest neglects the bishop's own summons. If a priest refers a case to a layman which he ought to refer to an ecclesiastic. If a priest neglects the archdeacon's summons. If a priest commits an offence and he celebrates mass in spite of the archdeacon's prohibition. If a priest refuses anyone baptism or confession. If a priest does not fetch the chrism at the proper time. We instruct that every child is to be baptized within nine days ... If a priest misdirect the people regarding a festival or fast. If a priest wrongly obtain ordination outside the diocese, ... he is to lose his orders, unless the bishop of the diocese acknowledges the ordination. If a priest consecrates mass in an unconsecrated building. If a priest consecrates mass without a consecrated altar. If the priest consecrates the host in a wooden chalice. If a priest celebrates mass without wine. If a priest neglects the host. If a priest celebrates mass more often than three times in one day ... If anyone wrongfully drives a priest from his church. If anyone wounds a priest. If anyone slays a priest. If a priest treats disrespectfully the church from which all his dignity must spring. If a priest puts unsuitable things in the church. If a priest removes church-goods. If a priest of his own free will deserts the church to which he was ordained. If a priest scorns or insults another by word or deed. If a priest fights another. If a priest gives assistance to wrong-doing. If a priest refuses lawful help to another. If a priest leaves another unwarned of what he knows will harm him. If a priest neglects the shaving of a beard or hair. If a priest leaves a woman and takes another. If a priest does not ring the hours nor sing the hours at the appointed time. If a priest comes with weapons into the church. If a priest performs in a wrong order the annual services of the church by day or night. If a priest conducts the ordeal wrongly. If a priest covers up fraud. If a priest practices drunkenness or becomes a glee-man or tavern-minstrel. If a priest conceals what wrong is rife among men in his parish. If a priest leaves the yearly dues undemanded. If a priest stays away from a synod. If a priest will not submit to what is right, but resists the bishop's ordinance.[13]

8) St. Thomas Becket

For my final medieval example of the priest in Anglicanism, I cite the one who has long been remembered as the patron saint of the clergy of England, St. Thomas Becket, the archbishop of Canterbury who was murdered in his own cathedral, whose martyrdom has long been seen as the highest ideal of a sacrifical priesthood: the good shepherd who gives his life for the sheep. There is probably no single hour in all the history of the Anglican church of which the details are so well known, and the true character of Christian priesthood so clearly delineated, as that time from about half-past two to half-past three on the afternoon of the 29th of December some eight and a quarter centuries ago, in 1170, when St. Thomas Becket, the archbishop of Canterbury, gave his life for the freedom of the church in England to criticize the sin and evil it perceived in the English government of that time. The story is told in accounts that are nearly contemporary.

The four knights in the service of King Henry II had entered Canterbury Cathedral that day and cried aloud: 'Where is the traitor, Thomas Becket?' When there was no reply, for Thomas denied it was treason to speak God's word boldly, they called again: 'Where is the archbishop?' Thomas then came forward: 'Here am I, no traitor, but a priest ready to suffer in my Redeemer's cause. God forbid that I should flee from your swords or depart from what is just. But do not dare to touch any of my people.' And then finally, as the sword fell that is said to have split his head and skull in two, he is recorded as paraphrasing these words of Holy Scripture: 'Into thy hands, O Lord, I commend my spirit. I accept death for the name of Jesus and for the Church.'

'Great he was, in truth, always and in all places,' wrote Herbert of Bosham, Becket's confidant and biographer. 'Great in the palace, great at the altar, great both at court and in the church; great when going forth on his pilgrimage, great when returning, and singularly great at his journey's end.'[14]

9) George Herbert

Moving on from the High Middle Ages, we now bridge the gulf of the great Reformation of the sixteenth century, saving the illustrious and formative theologian who concludes that period, Richard Hooker, for the second, and doctrinal, part of this essay. We remain, though, in the same Anglicanism that is continuous in essentials with the earliest church in the same land. The next Anglican description of priesthood I want to cite comes from George Herbert, the saintly rector of Fugglestone and Bemerton. It is his reflection juxtaposing Christian priesthood and the Old Testament priesthood of Exodus 28, in his poem called *Aaron*, published in 1633. The image of a priest vesting for Mass:

Holinesse on the head,
Light and perfections on the breast,
Harmonious bells below, raising the dead
To lead them unto life and rest.
Thus are true Aarons drest.

Profanenesse in my head,
Defects and darkness in my breast,
A noise of passions ringing me for dead
Unto a place where is no rest.
Poore priest thus am I drest.

Only another head
I have, another heart and breast,
Another musick, making live not dead,
Without whom I could have no rest:
In him I am well drest.

Christ is my only head,
My alone only heart and breast,
My only musick, striking me ev'n dead;
That to the old man I may rest,
And be in him new drest.

So holy in my head,
Perfect and light in my deare breast,
My doctrine tun'd by Christ, (who is not dead,
But lives in me while I do rest)
Come people; Aaron's drest.[15]

10) Charles Simeon

A quite different image of the priest in Anglicanism is conveyed by the great leader of the Evangelical movement in the Church of England, Charles Simeon, one of the founders of the Church Missionary Society, who died in 1833 as the Oxford Movement was just beginning. He speaks more of 'ministry' and 'ministrations,' though, than he does of 'priesthood,' although the New Testamental foundation of his imagery is the same. These are some of the words from his commentary on the ordinal in the Book of Common

Prayer, as he moves to a rebuke of a certain attitude in the English church of his own day.

> Let us pause for a moment to reflect what stress our Reformers laid on the Holy Scriptures as the only sure directory for our faith and practice and the only certain rule of all our ministrations. They have clearly given it as their sentiment that to study the word of God ourselves, and to open it to others, is the proper labor of a minister; a labor that calls for all his time and all his attention: and by this zeal of theirs in behalf of the Inspired Volume they were happily successful in bringing it into general use. But if they could look down upon us at this time and see what an unprecedented zeal has pervaded all ranks and orders of men amongst us for the dissemination of that truth, which they at the expense of their own lives transmitted to us; how would they rejoice and leap for joy!
>
> Yet, methinks, if they cast an eye upon this favored spot and saw that, whilst the Lord Jesus Christ is thus exalted in almost every other place, we are lukewarm in his cause; and whilst thousands all around us are emulating each other in exertions to extend his kingdom through the world, we, who are so liberal on other occasions, have not yet appeared in his favor; they would be ready to rebuke our tardiness.[16]

11) James Lloyd Breck

Closer now to home is the description of the discipline and formation for the Anglican priesthood in the early days of Nashotah House, the pioneer Anglo-Catholic seminary of the American midwest, which I have taken from two letters of James Lloyd Breck, its founder, written in 1842.

> Our dear Bishop has authorized us to purchase land and build a small house, and this we have accordingly done. We have purchased a tract of 460 acres of land on the Nashotah lakes, ten miles from Prairie Village, and yet more central to our Mission.

The students boarding with us are all theological, that is, those whom we intend for the Ministry. They are chiefly young men, sons of the farmers, and all communicants of the Church, save one that is too young, but is otherwise a Christian lad, who does a good deal of our housework. Our students, like ourselves, are poor, but not the less worthy for that. They seek the Ministry, but are unable to attain unto it without aid; and what aid can we give? We have a house; for this we pay no rent, – it belongs to the Church, and so do we. We have land; that is in like case; it is fertile beyond all calculation (that is to an Eastern man). They work four hours a day for their board and washing – and we give them their education without cost. Thus their clothing is their only expense; and to enable them to purchase this, we shall give them six weeks vacation during harvest, when they can earn the highest wages. In the winter they can split rails, for fencing in the spring. Our other students, not lay brethren of our House, will board with families nigh at hand, and pay for their tuition.

Brother Adams and myself work four hours, except when we are teaching or doing Missionary labor. We must all work for our board. This is the only way in which they will feel it their duty to labor and to study, and the only way in which our people will feel their duty to the Church, and to ourselves as the clergy of the same.

We rise at 5 a.m. Matins at 6. The Morning Service of the Church at 9. On Wednesdays and Fridays, the Litany at 12. On Thursdays the Holy Eucharist at the same hour of 12. The Evening Service of the Church at 3, and Family Prayer or Vespers at 6:30 or 7 p.m. Our students labor between 7 and 9 in the morning, and 1 and 3 in the afternoon.

Now that we are in a house of our own and the people see our readiness to undergo things unpleasant in themselves, they are made ready to bestow a portion of their produce on us.[17]

12) Alexander Forbes

The final piece I have chosen for this mosaic of 'The Priest in Anglicanism' is from *The Reminder of the Priestly Life*, originally written for Roman Catholic priests in France by Claude Arvisenet in 1794 but edited and translated for Anglican clergy in the mid-nineteenth century by the bishop of Brechin in Scotland, Alexander Forbes. Forbes had studied under John Keble at Oxford, had been a frequent visitor to Keble at Hursley vicarage, and was personally and successfully defended by Keble in a dispute over the doctrine of the Real Presence at Edinburgh in 1858. Forbes, as a disciple of Keble and son of the Oxford Reforms, had become especially beloved by the poor inhabitants of the slums of Dundee, where, during a cholera epidemic, he was to be found at all hours of the day and night, Prayer Book in one hand and a bottle of cholera medicine in the other. This selection from Alexander Forbes' English edition of *The Reminder of the Priestly Life*, on the difference between a spiritual priest and a worldly priest, represents in many ways the classical Anglo-Catholic ideal of priesthood. It haunts us, challenges us today, even if its language and terms are not always our own.

A worldly priest hath himself for an end, and looketh upon his ministry as an empty thing, except there come to him from it either honor or gain, or some temporal good.

But a spiritual priest, gifted with an upright heart, presseth forward to nothing earthly; but doeth all things purely for the sake of God and men's souls.

A worldly priest graspeth at rich benefices: he often complaineth of want, and straitened circumstances.

A spiritual priest committeth himself to God's good will: having food and raiment, he is therewith content.

A worldly priest carrieth his burden unwillingly: he feareth labor: he is slothful in study: he goeth not to the pulpit except when compelled. Those better than himself, wiser, more learned, more worthy, more rich, he envieth: he cannot endure the advice and the rebukes of his superiors.

But a spiritual priest liveth willingly in labor and in fatigue: he careth not for toils: his ecclesiastical superiors he obeyeth cheerfully: he restraineth his own liberty by the pious bonds of regular discipline. He desireth to be lord over none: but for the sake of God he is ready to take the last and lowest place.

A worldly priest desireth to be known, and to do that whence praise and admiration proceed.

But a spiritual priest, when he hath done all, attributes faithfully all the glory and honor to God: and for the rest, considereth himself an unprofitable servant.

A worldly priest, in his house, in his furniture, in his garments, seeketh for costly and fair things: the vile and common he disliketh.

But a spiritual priest is satisfied with simple and mean things: he avoideth the more costly and refined.

A worldly priest looketh out for a good stipend: he taketh delight in the gifts of his flock. He is sad if there be no recompense, if gain ceaseth, if any temporal loss ensue. He is irritated by contradiction, be it ever so little, or by the least injurious word.

But a spiritual priest regardeth eternal things alone: he careth not for temporal matters: he despiseth the world itself. He is not disturbed except for God being offended, or for souls being lost: by no harsh words is he aggrieved.

A worldly priest is stingy in giving, close in withholding.

But a spiritual priest, with a willing mind, becometh needy, so that the poor may live: he scattereth abroad, he giveth readily, cheerfully, abundantly.

A worldly priest desireth that what he hath done may be well considered. If he think that he hath conducted his actions well, then he wisheth to get his reward in this world. And if the Bishop doth not confer on him the reward either of some higher dignity or of some richer benefice, then he murmureth and complaineth within himself.

But a spiritual priest seeketh for nothing temporal: nor doth he ask for any other reward, as a return, but God alone.

O blessed, blessed, again and again, My son, is that priest, who is such as this.[18]

If I were to continue into this present century I would certainly want to cite and quote *The Christian Priest Today* by the late archbishop of Canterbury, Michael Ramsey, but limitations of space, and perhaps also the Tractarian principle of Reserve, bid me move on. So this concludes the mosiac of priests that I offer: the first recorded priest in Anglicanism who converted Alban, then the Venerable Bede, Aelfric, Wulfstan, Becket, George Herbert, Charles Simeon, James Lloyd Breck, Alexander Forbes, and of course Keble himself: ten very different examples, not exhaustive, but illustrative and evocative in quotations from their own words that reveal some of the ideals, some of the models, of 'The Priest in Anglicanism.' A diverse and attractive group of persons, but we may now ask, finally, wherein lies their unity?

Part II: The Anglican Doctrine of Priesthood

What I wish to develop in this second section of my essay is that there is a consistency and even unity of Anglican doctrine about priesthood, expressed of recent centuries in the Prayer Book and Ordinal, that underlies the diversity of persons who have been ordained to it and makes sense of the plurality of evidence that survives. It stretches back in essential continuity to the patristic period in which Anglicanism was born, and even earlier to the Holy Scriptures themselves. Here I shall attempt to expand upon what I have already written on this same subject.[19] My basic point is that, to arrive at the doctrine of 'The Priest in Anglicanism' which underlies all the various lives and ministries of persons who exemplify it, the Anglican tradition over the centuries has in fact accumulated five different sorts of priesthood all of which are interrelated in layers one upon another. To deal honestly with the evidence I believe it is necessary to resist the temptation of concluding, solely on the basis of logic, rather than fact, that because there is only one great high priest, Jesus Christ, there can therefore be only one sort of priesthood, his own, in the Christian church. The biblical, patristic, and historical evidence, all suggests otherwise. It is necessary now first to describe each of these five sorts of priesthood in some detail before I go on to show how their interrelationships constitute what I believe to be the Anglican doctrine of priesthood.

1) Number One – The Old Testament

The first priesthood to be considered is that found in the Hebrew scriptures of the Old Testament: the Levitical, cultic priesthood. These priests, called by the Hebrew noun *kohen*, were charged above all with offering sacrifices to God, to ensure the holiness of the nation as mediators of God's covenant with his people. Such a priest, at least by the time of Christ, was one who stood before God on behalf of the people at the altar of sacrifice. Such priests were born, not ordained or created in any other way, and hence the Old Testament priesthood was a sort of caste, hereditary in the tribe or house of Levi. Since, also, the tribe of Levi had no particular territory of its own assigned to it, these priests of the Old Testament were entitled to live on parts of the people's offerings to God, such as first-fruits, tithes, and payments for sacrifices. There are over seven hundred mentions of this first, cultic type of priesthood throughout the Old Testament.[20]

2) Number Two – Christ Himself

The next priesthood is that of Christ himself. Especially in the epistle to the Hebrews, Jesus is described as a priest (using the Greek word *hiereus*, the same word that translates the Hebrews *kohen* in the Septuagint Old Testament), but a unique priest in whom the Old Testament, cultic, sacrificial priesthood is understood to have been fulfilled, completed, and changed (cf. Heb. 7:12). He is believed to be the great high priest, one with the Father through his eternal sonship, yet by his incarnation identified with human beings, the perfect mediator of the New Covenant who has once for all made atonement for sin and opened for us a new and living way to union with God. He is, in fact, the only named person, apart from Jewish priests and one pagan functionary of the cult of Zeus at Lystra in Asia Minor, who in the New Testament is actually called *hiereus*. Jesus, then, is seen as in some ways like the priests of the Old Testament and in other ways unlike them. He was not, of course, born as one of them, but rather appointed by God; he is descended from Judah, not from Levi. He is said to hold his priesthood permanently, whereas the former priests were terminated in office by death (Heb. 7:23 – 24). He did offer a sacrifice propitiatory between the human race and God, yet the sacrificial victim he offered was not the blood of bulls and goats (alien blood that could never bring perfect union with God) but rather the body and blood of his own sinless life, a sacrifical offering anticipated in the Last Supper and consummated on Calvary. He was, therefore, seen as both priest and victim, and in his perfect sacrifice on the cross the Old Testament cultic priesthood is, for Christians, brought once and for all to a definitive conclusion.

We thus read of Christ in the epistle to the Hebrews: 'He has no need, like those high priests, to offer sacrifices daily, first for his own sins and then for those of the people; he did this once for all when he offered up himself' (Heb. 7:27). 'Every priest stands daily at his service, offering repeatedly the same sacrifices, which can never take away sins. But when Christ had offered for all time a single sacrifice for sins, he sat down at the right hand of God' (Heb. 10:11 – 12). Jesus Christ therefore comes to be described as 'our only mediator and advocate.' Whereas in the Old Covenant Aaron (depicted later so vividly for Anglicans in George Herbert's poem of the same name) was the representative figure of the high priesthood, the priesthood having its origin in Levi, so for the New Covenant the ideal type of Christ's priesthood is seen in the legendary figure of Melchizedek (Gen. 14:18, Ps. 110:4), who, we read in the epistle to the Hebrews, 'is without father or mother, or genealogy, and has neither beginning of days nor end of life' (Heb. 7:3). The priesthood of Christ, therefore, is totally unique. It is his priesthood, his sacrifice — 'one, full, perfect, and sufficient,' as the Anglican Prayer Book tradition puts it and as number 31 of the Thirty-Nine Articles affirms it — which is at the heart of the Christian gospel: the good news that he on the cross has done all that cultic sacrifices were unable to do, has reconciled humanity with divinity.

3) Number Three — The Church

A third sort of priesthood, now, is what we may call the priesthood of the church, of the total priestly people of God, the *laos tou theou*, 'the laity' (in the total meaning of this word), all those who, in Christian terms, are acknowledged as God's people by baptism. And this priesthood is designated in the New Testament Greek by a word closely related to *hiereus*, the word *hierateuma*. This is a priesthood characterized by the holiness of life to which the whole company of the faithful are called. This sort of priesthood, rather than deriving from the unique priesthood of Christ, is already anticipated and promised in such Old Testament passages as Isaiah 61:6: 'You shall be called the priests of the Lord; people shall speak of you as the ministers of our God,' or in Exodus 19:5–6: 'If you will obey my voice and keep my covenant, you shall be my own possession among all peoples, for all the earth is mine, and you shall be to me a kingdom of priests and a holy nation. These are the words which you shall speak to the children of Israel.'[21] It is this calling or election by God of the nation of Israel to be a holy and priestly people that certain New Testament writers properly see fulfilled in the corporate mission of the Christian church as a priestly people: 'You are a chosen race, a royal priesthood, a holy nation, a people of God's own possession, that you may show forth the wonderful deeds of him who called you out of darkness into his own marvelous light. Once you were no people at all, but now you are the people of God,' we read in I Peter 2:9–10, and earlier in the same letter we learn of the entire church's vocation 'to be a holy priesthood, to offer spiritual sacrifices acceptable to God through Jesus Christ.'

These spiritual sacrifices are not to be identified as the cultic sacrifices of the Old Testament, which are understood by Christians to have come to an end with Christ, nor as Christ's own sacrifice, which was offered once for all on the cross, nor as Christian eucharists, which are also of a different order as I shall suggest in a moment. Instead, these spiritual sacrifices which the entire Christian community is called by baptism to offer consist in the holy lives – 'our selves, our souls and bodies,' as the Prayer Book puts it – which we are to offer to God in thanksgiving for our justification and in witness to Christ and one another before the world in which we live. We, the elect and holy, now offer ourselves in holy living because of the life he lived, the sacrifice he offered. These spiritual sacrifices are, so to speak, a working out in an extended way of the ministry (*leitourgia*) that he once offered upon the cross, a making present now and at all times and in all places of his unique liturgy that was done once for all.[22] And so it is that in the book of Revelation those passages which describe, not the worship of heaven or the eschatological kingdom but the actual result here and now of the saving work of Christ, employ the language of priesthood in the same way, in terminology which reflects the promise to Israel given to Moses in Exodus 19:6. Thus we read: 'He has made of us a kingdom and priests for his God and Father' (Rev. 1:6); 'a kingdom and priests to our God, and they shall reign upon earth' (Rev. 5:10). This is the priesthood of the whole church, of all the people of God, a priesthood or 'liturgy' we especially attribute today to the non-ordained 'laity,' but a priesthood from which none of us, clergy or laity, are exempt, as we live out the liturgy of the cross in our daily lives.

Now we have considered three sorts of priesthood – Old Testament cultic priests, the unique priesthood of Christ, and the priesthood of the church – and we have in fact exhausted the biblical terminology of the Greek word for priest, *hiereus* (its Latin equivalent being *sacerdos*). But what about priests who have become 'priests' by ordination in Christ's one, holy, catholic, and apostolic church? The fact is, that no such persons are designated by the word *hiereus*, meaning 'priest', in the New Testament. What the New Testament does show, however, is that in addition to the priesthood of the whole church, and the vocation of every Christian to *diakonia*, or 'service' or 'ministry,' there is also 'another realm of the gifts of the Spirit,' as the 1973 Canterbury Statement on Ministry and Ordination from the Anglican-Roman Catholic International Commission put it, which has been poured forth by God in the Christian dispensation.[23] In Ephesians 4:11, for example, we read of apostles, prophets, evangelists, pastors, teachers; and in I Corinthians 12:8–10, 28–30, we read of healing, miracles, prophecy, discernment of spirits, tongues, interpretation of tongues. Still another such list is found in Romans 12:6–8: prophecy, service, teaching, exhortation, contributing, giving aid, doing acts of mercy. And in still other places we read of bishops or overseers, presbyters or elders, and deacons or servants (but not in any three-fold order this early). There are, in short, many offices, many gifts of the Spirit, within the general mission or ministry or priesthood of the whole church which exist to serve it and to build it up. Some of them had Old Testament parallels, some did not; some of them have continued down to this day, others were short-lived; some have become more institutionalized by ordination, others have been more spontaneous in nature; some may have been instituted directly by Christ, others by the church in obedience to what it thought was Christ's will. The way in which the ordained ministry has evolved from these New Testament complexities is described quite helpfully, I believe, in the same Canterbury Statement: 'The evidence suggests that with the growth of the Church the importance of certain functions led to their being located in specific officers of the community. Since the Church is built up by the Holy Spirit primarily but not exclusively through these ministerial functions, some form of recognition and authorization is already required in the New Testament period for those who exercise them in the name of Christ. Here we can see elements which will remain at the heart of what today we call ordination.'[24]

4) Number Four – Presbyters

And so we come to the fourth kind of priesthood that is necessary to be considered. It is constituted by one particular group of church office-holders, who came to be authorized or ordained, among the various sorts of persons within this special 'realm of the gifts of the Spirit': those who in the New Testament are called by the Greek term *presbyteroi*, meaning 'elders.' (Another group logically prior to them, the *episkopoi* or 'overseers' or 'bishops,' and their relationship to the original apostles as well as to the *presbyteroi*, is not the subject of this essay, but it is a topic that I have dealt with elsewhere.[25]) Let us now turn our attention to the group of church leaders called *presbyteroi*, because it is from them, from this Greek word by which they were called, that the fourth sort of priesthood emerges. The *presbyteros*, or presbyter, was a title borrowed from Jewish nomenclature to describe an elder male (the office was not open to women), a senior official, a prominent layperson, a community leader (soon, among Christians, without necessary reference to age), and was quite distinct from the Old Testament priestly families.

Most important, for the purpose of this present essay, is the fact that, in the Anglican tradition, in English-speaking Christianity, it is from the shortened Anglo-Saxon contraction of this word *presbyteros* that our English word 'priest' derives. (There are similar shortened forms in Spanish, French, Italian, German and Dutch). The point deserves emphasis: Although our English word 'priest' in virtually every English translation of the Bible is used to translate the Greek word *hiereus*, which means 'priest', our English word 'priest' is derived etymologically not from *hiereus* but from the Greek word *presbyteros*. And in the classical ordination rites of the western church, whether Roman Catholic or Anglican, it is by the Latin form of *presbyteros*, namely *presbyter*, that priests are called.[26] So the office or order we know in Anglicanism (and in Roman Catholicism) as that of a 'priest' was in origin that of a *presbyteros*, with all of the connotations that it entailed. Such *presbyteroi* did not come to be called 'priests' because they continue the Old Testament ritual priesthood, or because they are priests in the same sense that Jesus Christ was a *hiereus*, or because they derive their priesthood from the *hierateuma*, the priestly nature of the church as a whole, although all three of these priesthoods have left their marks upon them. They are priests, now in a fourth way: They are called priests because their name is the shortened English form of the Latin word *presbyter* or the Greek *presbyteros*.[27] This etymological distinction between *hiereus* and *presbyteros* has long been known in Anglican scholarship, the great student of the early church J.B. Lightfoot carefully noting in 1868 'the confusion between these two meanings [that] has affected the history and theology of the church.'[28]

One of the agreed conclusions of historical investigation and theological discussion emphasized as a cardinal point in the Canterbury Statement of the Anglican-Roman Catholic International Commission is the fact that this fourth sort of priesthood, the ordained presbyterate as it inheres in the Roman and Anglican churches today (and, we could add, in the Orthodox churches as well), belongs to a different 'realm of the gifts of the Spirit' from the third sort of priesthood, the priesthood or priestly nature of the whole church, prophesied in Exodus 19:5−6 and in Isaiah 61:6. *Presbyteroi*, that is to say, do not derive their priesthood, their priestliness, from the *hierateuma* of the whole church (even though they remain a part of it and in this sense partake also of its meaning), but rather their priesthood comes from being a Christian version, so to speak, of the Old Testament presbyterate. The common priesthood of the faithful and the ordained or hierarchical priesthood 'differ from one another in essence and not only in degree,' as the Second Vatican Council's dogmatic constitution on the church, *Lumen Gentium* (section 10), put it. In contrast to the Anglican tradition, it has been remarked, the churches of the complete Reformation generally came to equate these third and fourth sorts of priesthood, to reason from the priesthood of all believers, that is from the priestly

nature of the whole church, to the conclusion that every individual believer is therefore a priest.[29] The churches of the
complete Reformation, but not Anglicanism, thus came to
define the ordained priesthood (the ordained presbyterate)
as being simply a particular extension of the priesthood
(*hierateuma*) of all believers, rather than a conferral of the
presbyterate, and in this way the scriptural terminology was
confused and the distinction between the third and fourth
types of priesthoods was blurred. It is with this fourth sort
or type of priesthood, though, that the Anglican doctrine of
priesthood really begins, and I believe it is this doctrine that
is mirrored in John Keble's insistence upon the necessity of
episcopal ordination, rather than presbyteral, for the conferral of priesthood in the Church of England.

5) Number 5 – Priesthood Two Applied to Four

And yet there is still a fifth, and final, sort of priesthood,
which is really the application of priesthood number two
(that of Christ) to priesthood number four (the ordained
presbyterate) in order to serve priesthood number three (the
whole church), which is necessary for us to understand in
order to comprehend the full doctrine of the priest in Anglicanism. This is the application, beginning with many writers
of the early church, of the Greek word *hiereus* (or its Latin
equivalent *sacerdos*) to describe ordained Christian presbyters. (It was applied even earlier to Christian bishops,
but that is not the subject of this essay.) To use once
more the technical terms, (*episkopoi* and) *presbyteroi* are
not called *hiereis* in the New Testament, but by the early
third century A.D. they are beginning to be so called. In
short, the imagery of priesthood number two (the unique
priesthood of Christ), as well as some of the connotations
of the first and third sorts of priesthood, none of which the
New Testament identifies with the presbyterate or ordained
Christian priesthood, the fourth sort, come eventually to
be applied by analogy to it (and even earlier to the episcopate). And in this way there soon evolves a uniquely
Christian version of the Old Testament presbyterate. The
earliest Christian writers to do this, to make an application

of priesthood number two to number four, as I have culled them from Lampe's *Lexikon of Patristic Greek* and other sources, include the following (cited by exact or approximate year of death): Tertullian, 225; Hippolytus, 236; Origen, 254; Eusebius of Caesarea, 340; Basil of Caesarea, 379; Council of Constantinople, 381; Cyril of Jerusalem, 386; Gregory of Nazianzus, 390; Macarius of Egypt, 390; Gregory of Nyssa, 394; Didymus of Alexandria, 398; Apostolic Constitutions, fourth century.[30] Hence we find the origins of this process, of applying to presbyters (priests of the fourth sort) the priestly terminology used of Christ himself in the New Testament.

How, we may ask, did this come about? I think the following explanation is plausible. The Last Supper of Jesus with his disciples (in a pre-resurrection sense, the first eucharist) probably coincided with the celebration of a passover meal and at least shared many of its features. The one who first presided was Jesus himself, but as these meals continued after his death and resurrection the presiding officers very soon came to be the Christian bishops, or *episkopoi*, and then the presbyters or *presbyteroi* (priests in the fourth sense that I have outlined above) whom they appointed. St. Ignatius of Antioch, for example, writes to the Smyrnaeans in the early second century: 'You should regard that Eucharist as valid which is celebrated either by the bishop or by someone he authorizes.' But the eucharists that grew out of the Last Supper, which were quite different from the spiritual sacrifices of holy lives that all Christians as members of the priestly community called the church (the third sort of priesthood described above) were supposed to be leading, commemorated not only the original passover of the Old Testament but also, for Christians, the final sacrifice of Jesus himself, both priest (*hiereus* in the second sense) and victim.

Thus, by a sort of assimilation, or by a 'sacramental relation' as paragraph 13 of the Canterbury Statement puts it, or even by means of what we might call 'analogy' in classical theological language, but not by a simple univocal identification, the ordained Christian minister, the *presbyteros* (priest in the fourth sense), and of course even earlier the bishop, came in time to be called a *hiereus* as he was seen to be standing in the place of Christ. As Charles Price and Louis Weil put it in their volume *Liturgy for Living* in the Episcopal Church's Teaching Series (USA), the celebrant, or presider, at the Christian sacrifice came to be called a priest by the same derivative process whereby the eucharist itself came to be called a sacrifice.[31] In this way there was indicated the relationship of the presbyter (and bishop) to Christ who had presided at the Last Supper and the relationship of the Christian eucharist not only to the Last Supper but also to the sacrifice of Calvary vitally present in each eucharistic celebration.

This fifth sort of priesthood, then, is really an assimilation of the second priesthood, that of Christ, to the fourth one, the ordained presbyterate. It safeguards the ordained priest today from being seen simply as an elder, a senior official who has no commission directly from Christ and no responsibility directly to him, both of which safeguards are implied in the church's application of the term *hiereus* to the presbyter, in its use of priestly language for its ordained ministers. To say thus, as did F.D. Maurice in 1831/1842, that the ordained priest ministers on behalf of Christ to those who by baptism are already in a certain but different relationship to him, is to take neither the classical 'protestant' view that because Christ is a priest there can be no human priesthood, nor the extreme 'catholic' view that the priest acts vicariously in place of a Christ who is totally absent from his church on earth.[32] Let us see how this development of a fifth, and final, sort of priesthood is described by various modern commentators, and is located by them in a eucharistic context.

Let us first cite once more a great accomplishment of the modern ecumenical movement, the Canterbury Statement of the Anglican-Roman Catholic International Commission. The process of assimilation of priesthood number two to priesthood number four, so extensively discussed in its deliberations, may well have led its compilers to write these words in their thirteenth paragraph: 'Despite the fact that in the New Testament ministers are never called 'priests' (*hiereis*), Christians came to see the priestly role of Christ reflected in these ministers and used priestly terms in describing them. Because the Eucharist is the memorial of the sacrifice of Christ, the action of the presiding minister in reciting again the words of Christ at the last supper and distributing to the assembly the holy gifts is seen to stand in a sacramental relation to what Christ himself did in offering his own sacrifice. So our two traditions commonly use priestly terms in speaking about the ordained ministry.'

Price and Weil make the same point, it seems, but more succinctly, when they say: 'In the course of the third century, the title *priest* was given to bishops, and eventually it fell to presbyters, also, because bishops and presbyters presided at the Eucharist, which made Christ's sacrifical death present to the worshipping community and its effects available to the church.'[33] And Richard Hooker in the late sixteenth century had already made a similar evaluation of the patristic development in his *Ecclesiastical Polity*: 'The Fathers of the Church of Christ with like security of speech call usually the ministry of the Gospel *Priesthood* in regard of that which the Gospel hath *proportionable* to ancient sacrifices, namely the Communion of the blessed Body and Blood of Christ, although it have properly now no sacrifice.'[34]

A final comment upon the process that led to this fifth and fullest sort of ordained priesthood in Anglican understanding comes from the introduction to *Prayer Book Studies 20*, a semi-official volume published in preparation for the new American Prayer Book of 1979. It describes the second order of ordained ministry as being both presbyteral, which is the sort I have called priesthood number four, and sacerdotal, which is the kind I have called priesthood number two: 'As presbyteral Priests, clergymen are called to work under the leadership of their Bishop and with one another in the second order of the ordained ministry. As sacerdotal Priests, they are to pronounce absolution and blessing, and officiate at the altar, doing so, not merely as the licensed deputies of the Bishop, but as the ordained representatives of Christ. In Anglican tradition, members of the second order of ministry are also called to be pastors and teachers as well as priests, but the

English word, priest, has come to contain all these meanings.'[35]

6) Nine Conclusions

With the fifth and final of these sorts of priesthood I think the Anglican doctrine is complete, and it is now time to draw some conclusions. Much of this account is a story that has been told in the telling, as the saying goes, but I do think some crisp concluding observations about the fifth of these priesthoods, the doctrine of the priest in Anglicanism, can be offered. For brevity and convenience I will number them:

1) The relationship of priesthood number five to priesthood number one (of the Old Testament) is by means of typology, as George Herbert's poem *Aaron* underlines in a poetical way ('Only another head I have, another heart and breast ... Christ is my only head, My alone only heart and breast ... Come people; Aaron's drest'). Aaron, the representative figure of the Old Testament high priesthood, is the 'type' not of Christ or of Melchizedek, but of the ordained Christian presbyter who is called a priest in the sense of number five.

2) Priesthood number five is a development from number four (the presbyterate), and therefore such a person is properly called 'priest' rather than merely 'presbyter,' although at times it is desirable to call such priests 'presbyters' in order to distinguish them from number two (Christ himself) or even from number one (the Old Testament sort of priesthood). In the Anglican tradition 'priest' is the Prayer Book's standard term for them, and Price and Weil remark: 'This usage of the word *priest* has been accepted in Eastern Orthodox, Roman Catholic, and Anglican churches.'[36] It is misleading, although technically accurate, to describe one who has been ordained to priesthood number five as a 'presbyter,' with no remainder.

3) The purpose of priesthood number five, which is an assimilation or application to number four (the presbyterate) of the priestly terminology reserved to Christ in number two, is to serve priesthood number three (the whole church). This is well put in section seven of the Canterbury Statement where

we read that 'The goal of the ordained ministry is to serve this priesthood of all the faithful.' Thus we may say that just as eucharistic presidency is historically and theologically the distinctive priestly act, so the eucharist itself is that which defines and actualizes the church.

4) The purpose of both number five and number three (the whole church) is, obviously, to serve number two (Christ himself). The church also, it needs to be said, is not an end in itself, but is directly subservient to the One who is its Head.

5) Sacramental priests of the sort that I have labelled number five, which is what an Anglican or Episcopal priest in the last analysis is, retain membership in number three (the whole church), but do not derive their priesthood from it. Of course, such priests do not cease to be laity once they are ordained, and they act *in persona ecclesiae* in the leadership of the church's prayers as well as in other functions; but their function as representatives of the laity does not exhaust that which is conferred upon them sacramentally at ordination. This is the point of Keble's insistence upon episcopal rather than presbyteral ordination, as well as of Vatican II's *Lumen Gentium* (section 10) which I have already cited. They are priests by analogy to Christ (number two), while at the same time exercising leadership functions in the priestly body (number three). And because number five retains membership in number three, for example, any standards of conduct agreed as being appropriate to number three must automatically apply also, as a minimum, to number five.

6) Priesthood number five as well as priesthood number three are both representative of Christ, yet in different but overlapping ways. The new Anglican catechism of the 1979 Book of Common Prayer of the Episcopal Church in the U.S.A. makes this distinction on pp. 855–856. When it connects the sense in which the priest (or presbyter, but in the sense of number five) 'represents Christ' with the ministry of the priest to administer the sacraments and to bless and declare pardon in God's name (p. 856), it is standing in the catholic theological tradition that has described the priest as *alter Christus*, 'another Christ,' and the priest's

ministry in this regard as one exercised *in persona Christi*, 'in the person of Christ.' (*cf*. II Corinthians 2:10).

7) Priesthood number five represents priesthood number two (Christ) to priesthood number three (the whole church) in the manner of an icon, but as a fellow member of the laity number five also represents priesthood number three (the church) to number two (Christ, or God in Christ) by way of leadership in prayer (*in persona ecclesiae*). Thus the priest exercises a dual role in the eucharist, sometimes representing the people and at other times representing Christ.[37] The Episcopal Church's Book of Common Prayer (pp. 334, 362) directs the eucharistic celebrant to hold or lay hand upon the bread and upon the cup while saying Jesus' words of institution in the eucharistic prayer as the narrative itself switches from third person to first person, thus conveying visually and verbally an image of Christ at the table of the Last Supper, rather than merely reading Jesus' words from the lectern or pulpit or elsewhere.[38] In this way, then, the eucharistic celebration, certainly in the great thanksgiving if not already in the offertory, makes a public and powerful visual statement of the consistent doctrine of priesthood that follows the tradition of earlier Anglican Prayer Books begun in 1549 by causing the priest (number five) to appear and function here as an icon or image of Christ. This dual role of the priest in the eucharist was well expressed by the 1976 Moscow Statement of the international Anglican-Orthodox Joint Doctrinal Commission: 'The celebrant, in his liturgical action, has a twofold ministry: as an icon of Christ, acting in the name of Christ towards the community and also as a representative of the community expressing the priesthood of the faithful.'[39]

8) The action and appearance of the priest (number five) as an icon or image of Christ in the eucharist is done by way of *anamnesis*, or vital recall, rather than by *mimesis*, or physical impersonation. The less emphasis there is upon the personal, in fact, the greater is the opportunity for the *anamnesis* to be evident. The priest is clearly seen here as an *alter Christus* acting *in persona Christi*, but the fact that the iconography occurs by way of *anamnesis* guards against the necessity for a literal identification of the priest with

number one or number two — that is, with Christ's mas-
culinity (or with other physical resemblances that might be
imagined, such as a beard). It allows for women as well as
men to represent Christ as ordained priests (number five).
At the same time it leaves room for the priest's many other
actions *in persona ecclesiae* (in the person of the church), for
example in leading the people's prayers that are addressed
to the Divinity on their behalf, as well as in many pastoral
ministrations that are carried out day by day.

9) The application of priesthood number two (that of
Christ) to the ordained presbyterate of number four,
whereby number five is produced, is admittedly a post-
scriptural development of the early church, but this is
not a problem for churches in the catholic tradition that
Anglicanism shares, if critically, with the Roman Catholic
and Orthodox churches. By the Chicago-Lambeth Quadrilateral of 1886–88, for example, the Episcopal Church in the
United States, and indeed the entire Anglican Communion,
is committed to the legitimacy of such post-scriptural developments as a fixed canon of Scripture, the Apostles' and
Nicene creeds, a sacramental understanding of baptism and
eucharist, and the 'historic' episcopate. All of these Anglicanism consistently defends as being appropriate extensions
and developments of the foundational scriptural witness,
so long as they confirm it and do not distort it, and the
same is true of the sacramental priesthood (number five).[40]
Lightfoot, later bishop of Durham, had in 1868 and thus
before the Quadrilateral was framed, already acknowledged
and reckoned with this development in the use of the word
'priest' when he observed that 'The appearance of this phe-
nomenon marks the period of transition from the universal
sacerdotalism of the New Testament to the particular sacerdotalism of a later age.' He concluded, however, that
'if the word be taken in a wider and looser acceptation,
it cannot well be withheld from the ministry of the Church
of Christ.'[41]

These observations now conclude my survey of the doctrine of the priest in Anglicanism, a survey that of course
does not cover every point of the doctrine although I believe
it does trace the main lines of development. The doctrine is

a remarkably consistent one reaching back to Scripture and the earliest sources and remaining in essentials unchanged even through the transitional period of the sixteenth century emergency, a doctrine lived and defended in the ministry and writing of John Keble, a doctrine that does undergird all the varied and manifold priestly lives who have ministered under its authority.

Notes

1. John Keble, *The Christian Year: Thoughts in Verse for the Sundays and Holydays throughout the Year*, 1st American ed., (Philadelphia: Carey, Lea and Blanchard, 1834), 12.
2. *The Alternative Service Book 1980: Services Authorized for Use in the Church of England in Conjunction with The Book of Common Prayer* (London: Central Board of Finance of the Church of England, 1980), 19.
3. J. Keble, *Lyra Innocentium*, as reprinted in *The Mind of the Oxford Movement*, ed. Owen Chadwick (London: Adam and Charles Black, 1960), 144.
4. *The Works of that Learned and Judicious Divine, Mr. Richard Hooker: with an Account of his Life and Death by Isaac Walton*, ed. John Keble, 6th ed. (Oxford: Clarendon Press, 1874), 1:1xi, 1xxvi – 1xxvii; *cf. ibid.*, 3:231 – 32.
5. I have surveyed this and other evidence in 'Anglicanism, *Ecclesia Anglicana*, and Anglican: An Essay on Terminology,' in *The Study of Anglicanism*, ed. Stephen Sykes and John Booty (London and Philadelphia: SPCK and Fortress Press, 1988), 424 – 29.
6. For a good discussion of the evidence, see Arthur Swinson, *The Quest for Alban* (St Albans: The Fraternity of the Friends of St. Albans Abbey, 1971), esp. p. 40. On the date of Alban's martyrdom, see also Charles Thomas, *Christianity in Roman Britain to AD 500* (Berkeley and Los Angeles: University of California Press, 1981), 42 – 44, 48 – 50.
7. Bede, *Historia Ecclesiastica* I.7.
8. The author is John Ernest Bode, and the publisher, J.H. Parker of Oxford.
9. Bede, *Historia Ecclesiastica* V.24.
10. *The Proper for the Lesser Feasts and Fasts, 1991* (New York: The Church Hymnal Corporation, 1991), 230.
11. Anglo-Saxon text and English translation in *Councils and Synods with Other Documents Relating to the English Church*, ed. D. Whitelock, M. Brett, and C.N.L. Brooke (Oxford: Clarendon Press, 1981) 1:191 – 226.
12. *Ibid.*, 422 – 27.

13. *Ibid.*, 449–68.
14. Account reconstructed and translated from primary sources by M.D. Knowles in *Archbishop Thomas Becket: A Character Study* (London: Geoffrey Cumberlege, 1949/1970), 21–23. My summary here is paraphrased from this Raleigh Lecture on History, 1949, from the Proceedings of the British Academy, vol. 35.
15. From Herbert's larger work, *The Temple: the Church.*
16. Charles Simeon, *The Excellency of the Liturgy* (London, 1812), excerpted in *Prayer Book Spirituality*, ed. J. Robert Wright (New York: The Church Hymnal Corporation, 1989), 444. I have made some modernization.
17. *The Life of the Reverend James Lloyd Breck, D.D., chiefly from Letters written by Himself*, ed. Charles Breck, 3rd ed. (New York: 1886), 29, 33–34; *cf. James Lloyd Breck: Apostle of the Wilderness*, ed. Thomas C. Reeves (Nashotah, 1992), 50–51, 54–55. I have made some ellipsis for the sake of brevity.
18. *Memoriale Vitae Sacerdotalis, or Solemn Warnings of the Great Shepherd Jesus Christ to the Pastors of His Church*, 'from the Latin of Arvisenet. Adapted to the Use of the Anglican Church by the Bishop of Brechin.' 2nd ed. (London: Joseph Masters, 1873), 23–29. I have made some ellipsis for the sake of brevity.
19. See especially my 'The Canterbury Statement and the Five Priest-hoods,' in *One in Christ* 11 (1975): 282–93, and (with slight variations) in *Anglican Theological Review* 57 (October 1975): 446–56. In these earlier articles I drew out the implications for Anglican-Roman Catholic relations at greater length than is possible in the present essay.
20. Some of my information here is derived from *The Interpreter's Dictionary of the Bible*, ed. G.A. Buttrick *et al.* (New York and Nashville: Abingdon Press, 1962), 3:876–91; and its supplementary volume, ed. Keith Crim (Nashville: Abingdon, 1976), 687–90; as well as from William F. Arndt and F. Wilbur Gingrich, *A Greek-English Lexicon of the New Testament and Other Early Christian Literature* (Chicago: University of Chicago Press, and Cambridge: Cambridge University Press, 1957), esp. p. 372. I am also indebted to Professor Richard Corney of The General Theological Seminary, New York, for helpful assistance.
21. This is a point made, for example, by John Hall Elliott, *The Elect and the Holy* (Leiden: E.J. Brill, 1966), 220; and by Raymond E. Brown, *Priest and Bishop* (Paramus, N.J.: Paulist Press, 1970), 14–15 (*cf.* his review of Elliott in *Catholic Biblical Quarterly* 29 [1967]: 255–57); and by Jean M.R. Tillard, *What Priesthood Has the Ministry?* (Bramcote, Nottingham: Grove Booklet no. 13, 1973), and also in *One in Christ* 9 (1973): 237–69; the French original was published in *Nouvelle Revue Théologique* (May 1973): 481–514. See, in addition, J.M.R. Tillard, 'Sacerdoce,' in *Dictionnaire de Spiritualité Ascétique et Mystique, Doctrine et Histoire* (Paris: Beauchesne, 1990), 14: cols. 2–11. For the influence of Exodus 19:5–6 and

Isaiah 61:6 upon this concept of the priesthood of the church, see *Theological Dictionary of the New Testament* ed. G. Kittel (Grand Rapids: Eerdmans Publishing Co., 1965), 3:249, 264.

22. This point is well developed by Charles P. Price and Louis Weil, *Liturgy for Living* (New York: The Seabury Press, 1979), 21–24 and *cf.* 42–43. Further, see Tillard, 'Sacerdoce,' op.cit., cols. 22–26.

23. Para 13. See also Alan C. Clark, *Ministry and Ordination: The Statement on the Doctrine of the Ministry Agreed by the Anglican/Roman Catholic International Commission, Canterbury, 1973: The Official Text, Together with an Introduction and Commentary* (Pinner, Middlesex, England: Catholic Information Office, 1974); and also Julian Charley, *Agreement on the Doctrine of the Ministry: The 1973 Anglican/Roman Catholic Statement on Ministry and Ordination (with Historical Appendix), with Theological Commentary and 'Notes on Apostolic Succession'* (Bramcote, Nottingham: Grove Booklet no. 22, 1973). I am especially indebted to these works, as well as to those of J.M.R. Tillard referenced in note 21 above, for my interpretation of the Canterbury Statement.

24. Para. 5.

25. 'The Origins of the Episcopate and Episcopal Ministry in the Early Church,' in *On Being a Bishop: Papers on Episcopacy from the Moscow Consultation 1992*, ed. J. Robert Wright (New York: The Church Hymnal Corporation, 1993), 10–32.

26. H.B. Porter, Jr. *The Ordination Prayers of the Ancient Western Churches* (London: SPCK, 1967), 8, 10, 26; *Pontificale Romanum Summorum Pontificum* (Mechlin, Belgium: H. Dessain, 1895), 55*ff*; *Ordinations* (Techny, Illinois: Divine Word Publications, 1942), 95*ff* and esp. 115. *The Treatise on the Apostolic Tradition of St. Hippolytus of Rome*, ed. G. Dix and revised by H. Chadwick (London: SPCK, 1968), 13, shows *presbyteros* in the Greek text. The new Roman Pontifical reads 'Da, quaesumus, omnipotens Pater, in hos famulos tuos Presbiterii dignitatem;' see *Pontificale Romanum ex Decreto Sacrosancti Oecumenici Concilii Vaticani II Instauratum Auctoritate Pauli PP. VI Promulgatum. De Ordinatione Diaconi, Presbyteri, et Episcopi.* Editio Typica (Vatican: 1968), 44. Some Latin versions of The Book of Common Prayer read 'Ad officium et munus presbyteri,' whereas others read 'In officium et opus sacerdotis.' See also *Anglican Orders (English): The Bull of His Holiness Leo XIII, September 13, 1896, and the Answer of the Archbishops of England, March 29, 1897* (London: SPCK, 1957), 18, 40–45; and *Anglican Orders (Latin)* (London: SPCK, 1932), 36–40.

27. Richard A. Norris, Jr., has put it this way: 'The English term 'priest' is merely a syncopation of the Greek *presbuteros*, 'elder'. . . . In popular parlance, 'priest' means a Roman Catholic, Eastern Orthodox, or possibly even Anglican, cleric who is habitually pre-occupied with rites, ceremonies, sacraments and sacrifices; and even among the learned it is understood that the English 'priest' renders

hiereus and *sacerdos* as well as *presbuteros;*' see R.A. Norris, Jr., 'The Beginnings of Christian Priesthood,' in *Anglican Theological Review* 66, supplementary series no. 9 (1984): 19.

28. J.B. Lightfoot, *The Christian Ministry*, ed. Philip Edgcumbe Hughes (Wilton, Connecticut: Morehouse-Barlow, Inc., 1983), 32. This work was originally published in 1868 as an appendix to Lightfoot's commentary on *Philippians*.

29. Tillard, *What Priesthood Has the Ministry?*, op.cit., is the seminal study on this point; *cf.* esp. his remarks on pp. 27–28. See also *The Priesthood of the Ordained Ministry*, published by the Board for Mission and Unity of the General Synod of the Church of England (London: Church House Publishing, 1986).

30. *A Patristic Greek Lexicon*, ed. G.W.H. Lampe (Oxford: Clarendon Press, 1961), 670. A helpful survey and discussion is given by Tillard, *What Priesthood ...?*, op.cit., 20–25. See also Kittel, 3:283; D.N. Power, *Ministers of Christ and His Church* (London: Geoffrey Chapman, 1969), 38–39, 67, 82–85, 101–07; Hans Küng, *The Church* (New York: Sheed and Ward, 1967), 364–66, 382–87; Jaroslav Pelikan, *The Emergence of the Catholic Tradition*, (Chicago: University of Chicago Press, 1971), 1:25, 160; and J. Blenkinsopp, 'Presbyter to Priest: Ministry in the Early Church,' *Worship* 41 (August-September 1967): 428–38. For a recent scholarly treatment of this material and its development, see Tillard, 'Sacerdoce,' op.cit., cols. 12–22.

31. Price and Weil, 42.

32. F.D. Maurice, *The Kingdom of Christ*, ed. Alec R. Vidler (London: S.C.M. Press, Ltd., 1958), 2:148. This work was originally published in London in 1838.

33. Price and Weil, 281.

34. *Of the Laws of Ecclesiastical Polity*, V.78.2, excerpted in *Prayer Book Spirituality*, ed. J. Robert Wright (New York: The Church Hymnal Corporation, 1989), 432. Anthony Sparrow, Bishop of Norwich in the mid-seventeenth century, is cognizant of the same development that applied what I have called priesthood number two to number four in order to produce number five, but he is less precise in describing it; the pertinent passages from his *Rationale upon The Book of Common Prayer* are excerpted in the above, 432–33.

35. *The Ordination of Bishops, Priests, and Deacons: Prayer Book Studies 20* (New York: The Church Hymnal Corporation, 1970), 11.

36. Price and Weil, 43.

37. This dual representation is brought out well in the article by Julia Gatta, 'The Marriage of the Bride and the Lamb: The Celebrant's Prayer in the Eucharist' in *Sewanee Theological Review* 35 (1992): 173–81, to which I am indebted for helpful suggestions.

38. Hence the protest of Hooker that 'some, when they labour to shew the use of the holy Sacraments, assign unto them no end but only

to teach the mind, by other senses, that which the Word doth teach by hearing;' see *Of the laws of Ecclesiastical Polity*, V.57.1.

39. Para. 27.

40. Further, see my book *Quadrilateral at One Hundred* (Cincinnati: Forward Movement Publications, and London and Oxford: Mowbray, 1988). The post-scriptural development whereby the order of diaconate has come to be included as a necessary foundation for the ordained priestly ministry of number five is a subject I have recently treated elsewhere at great length; see my 'Sequential or Cumulative Orders vs: Direct Ordination' in *Anglican Theological Review* 75 (Spring 1993): 246–51, and also my 'Richard Hooker and the Doctrine of Cumulative or Sequential Orders' in *Sewanee Theological Review* 36 (Easter 1993); 246–51.

41. Lightfoot, 106, 113.

The Pastor in Anglicanism

The Oxford Movement of which the shy, reserved, self-effacing John Keble was recognised as first leader has still an awesomeness, a numinous power, which makes one speak of it with bated breath. In its depths it was a Holiness Movement. Its effects on *Ecclesia Anglicana* and its world-wide progeny are enduring. But it has not only made history; it has re-written it and not least by misunderstanding the Protestant Reformation and underplaying its influence, in the attempt to affirm the catholicity of the English church and to trace a continuity from the beginnings of Christianity, obscure as they may be. This needs to be said at the start.

Romanticism, not to be disparaged, may see the exemplar of the Anglican pastoral tradition in Chaucer's 'Poure Persoun of a Toun':

> This noble ensample to his sheepe he yaf
> That firste he wroghte and afterward he taughte ...
> ... Cristes loore and his apostles twelve,
> He taughte, but first he folwed it hymselve.

The roots are in the New Testement itself and certainly may be found in Theodore of Tarsus, archbishop of Canterbury from 668 to 690. He not only remodelled the diocesan framework of the English church, but adopted the Celtic penitential system, with its conception of penance as medicinal rather than punitive; this in contrast to the Roman. But the soil in which the tradition was re-planted was the Reformation.[1] This is manifest in the Prayer Book Ordinal. In their reply to the papal condemnation of Anglican orders in *Apostolicae Curae*, the English archbishops, in 1897, commented that the English Reformers

> saw that the duties of the pastoral office had but little place in the Pontifical, although the Gospel speaks out

fully upon them. For this reason then they especially
set before our Priests the pastoral office, which is
particularly that of Messenger, Watchman and Steward
of the Lord, in that noble address which the Bishop has
to deliver, and in the very serious examination which
follows: in words which must be read and weighed and
compared with the holy Scriptures, or it is impossible
really to know the worth of our Ordinal.[2]

In the earliest works of pastoral theology, there is little to
choose between those called Puritans and the others. Some
modern scholars would confine the name Puritan to those
clergymen and members of the Church of England before
1640, who, like the majority, were Calvinist in theology,
but wished to reform the church further in the directions of
Calvinist polity and liturgy. There is evidence that for John
Bunyan, for instance, at any rate by 1680, 'Puritan' was a
term of the past.[3] Be that as it may, H.R. McAdoo in *The
Structure of Caroline Moral Theology* finds himself quoting
Richard Baxter several times, Baxter who is considered the
greatest of the Puritans by those who would extend the
description to the Nonconformists of 1662.[4] But Baxter was
in deacon's orders, his priesthood is uncertain, though he was
offered the bishopric of Hereford in 1661. He was the author
of the Savoy liturgy, intended with a certain over-optimistic
presumptuousness to be an eirenical alternative to the Prayer
Book, and which, of course, pleased nobody. It comes near
to a doctrine of eucharistic sacrifice and offering beyond
that of Cranmer, as well as retaining actions omitted from
1552. His conscience meant that he had to join the ejected
in 1662, but at Kidderminster during the Commonwealth he
had exercised a remarkable pastoral ministry, which came far
to making the whole town Christian. Bishop Hensley Henson
of Durham said, when unveiling a tablet to Baxter's memory
in 1925, that his book *The Reformed Pastor* (1656) 'is the
best manual of a clergyman's duty in the language, because
it leaves on the reader's mind an ineffaceable impression of
the sublimity and awfulness of spiritual ministry.'[5] Baxter
in many ways filled the ideals of George Herbert for whom
he had the greatest admiration. 'He speaks to *God* like one

that *really believeth a God*, and whose business in the world is most with God. Heart-work and Heaven-work make up his Books.'[6]

Herbert's *The Countrey Parson His Character and Rule of Holy Life*, of which the main title *A Priest to the Temple* may be an editorial addition, was first published in 1652, nineteen years after Herbert's death. It is the first work of what would now be called Anglican pastoral theology.[7] Herbert's loyalty to the established church was undoubted, and he saw it as the via media between what Simon Patrick saucily called 'the meretricious gaudiness of Rome and the squalid sluttery of fanatic conventicles', though Herbert's language in his poem 'The British Church' is gentler. Izaak Walton's life of Herbert is now considered to be misleading in several ways, too hagiographical, though no one could doubt Herbert's sancity, and unaware of the turbulence of his spiritual struggles. Herbert's theology was Lutheran-Calvinist, and Richard Strier has suggested that 'the devotional and theological temper of men like John Cotton, John Downame and Richard Sibbes was in many ways closer to Herbert's than was that of Richard Hooker, Archbishop Laud or even Lancelot Andrewes.'[8]

We should notice, among the so-called Puritans, Richard Greenham, rector of Dry Drayton, Cambridge, whose ministry though much longer (1570–90), twenty years as against three, resembled that of George Herbert at Bemerton from 1630. He seems to have been a minister of kindly and gentle disposition, earnest and grave, austere in self-discipline and the keeping of Sabbaths, a Sabbatarian in fact, but tender with his flock, and as able to draw an illustration from the sights and sounds of his village cure as to plumb the depths of the subconscious mind. He was a true physician of the afflicted conscience and a private counsellor, or confessor, as well as a preacher. The title 'soul-friend' might have been invented for him.

One cannot read Herbert today without being aware of the social status from which the parson ministered, reinforced by the establishment. There was no 'identity crisis', or doubt as to his place in the community. He might be social worker, physician of the body and legal advisor too. But he would rule is own household and walk about his parish with every right to reprove, admonish and commend. Small talk was not expected. He was there to enquire as to spiritual states and religious practices. He was the man of God, the vicegerent of Christ, the reconciler of differences, the arbiter in disputes, the one with a duty to denounce a delinquent to the law for his punishment, yet to treat him still as a brother and not to change 'his behaviour and carriage towards him'. He were better celibate since virginity is a higher state than matrimony, yet marriage is less dangerous, with fewer temptations; and a wife, chosen by the ear rather than the eye, will assist his ministry in the parish as 'a beginner of good discourses', train up children and maids in the fear of God, 'with prayers and catechizing and all religious duties', be a nurse, 'curing and healing all wounds and sores with her own hands', and skilled in household management, keeping good accounts. 'His children he first makes Christians, then commonwealth's men'. He teaches them prayer and reading, but also good works in bestowing charity, sometimes from their own pockets. He gives to the eldest son 'the perogative of his father's profession' and the rest are not to be put into vain trades 'unbefitting the reverence of their father's calling, such as are taverns for men and lace-making for women'. The servants must all be religious and are taught not only truth, diligence and neatness and cleanliness, but also reading and given time to read. 'His family is a school of religion' and 'in the house of a preacher all are preachers'.

He never behaves anywhere as other than a priest. Prayer accompanies everything. His 'library is a holy life'. He is generally sad, 'because he knows nothing but the Cross of Christ, his mind being defixed on it with those nails wherewith his master was: or if he have leisure to look off from thence, he meets continually with two most sad spectacles, sin and misery; God dishonoured every day and man afflicted'. But 'nature will not bear everlasting droopings, and ... pleasantness of disposition is a great key to do good'. He therefore 'intermingles some mirth in his discourses', though one feels more as a concession to human frailties than as a share in the joy of God. He seeks to turn all to God's Providence, adversity and prosperity, the vagaries as well as the abundance of nature. Preaching is central, even though in 'The Church Porch', Herbert, the poet, says that praying's best. But 'the country parson preacheth constantly, the pulpit is his joy and his throne.' There is counsel on the composition and style of sermons. They should be fairly short, no more than an hour. They should be expositions of Scripture. Herbert was steeped in the Bible, as is clear from a close examination of his poems. Seventeenth-century Protestants lived in the Bible. 'Israelite history became a kind of map on which believers could plot their own spiritual position.'[9] Herbert seems to tilt at the style of Lancelot Andrewes when he advises against 'crumbling a text into small parts', which is to treat Scripture like a dictionary. The character of the sermon must be holiness. The chosen texts should be of devotion not controversy; preaching should be from the heart and with frequent apostrophes to God as in the prophets; it must reflect a Pauline care and joy in the people's salvation and always with 'an urging of the presence of God' in his majesty and mercy. Catechizing is essential as well as preaching. This is the preferred method of education and preaching's vital accompaniment. But 'questions cannot inflame or ravish'. This can be done only by the sermon.

It must be borne in mind that preaching was far more frequent in the seventeenth-century church than the eucharist. In the poem 'Aaron,' Herbert is thinking more of vesting for the pulpit than the altar – 'my doctrine tuned by Christ'. And as McAdoo insists, preaching was the principal method of spiritual direction.[10]

Herbert most certainly reverenced the sacraments. In baptism he is clothed in white. He is reluctant to administer it except on Sundays or great days. He will allow 'no vain or idle names'. He uses the sign of the cross as 'not only innocent but reverend'. Here he differed from the Puritans, who feared it might distract from the water-ceremony and confuse people as to what baptism actually was. Like the Puritans, he asks Christians to meditate on their baptism. The sacrament of Holy Communion must be observed with reverence and solemnity.[11] There must be preparation, aided by comparative infrequency. Herbert would have wished for once a month; otherwise 'at least five or six times a year, as at Easter, Christmas, Whitsuntide, afore and after harvest, and the beginning of Lent'. He admits that there is some proper dispute over the manner of receiving. 'The feast indeed requires sitting, because it is a feast; but man's unpreparedness asks kneeling. He that comes to the Sacrament has the confidence of a guest, and he that kneels confesseth himself an unworthy one, and therefore differs from other feasters; but he who sits and lies puts up to an Apostle: contentiousness in a feast of charity is more scandal than any posture'. Herbert is not doctrinaire in this nor in anything, though he prefers kneeling and the Laudian arrangement of the church. His poem 'The Invitation' seems to presume that worshippers will draw near to partake of the feast – 'Come ye hither,' that is to the altar at the east end. He did not wish for undue ornamentation of the building, but for a clean and light plainness; and to kneel was in penitence and humility, not in adoration of the sacred species.

We must now turn to the great seventeenth-century casuists, who, again cannot be rigidly separated in moral theology from the Puritans, who like them were fascinated by the Schoolmen and not only borrowed but stole. John Preston, Master of Emmanuel Cambridge, read Aquinas at the barber's. 'If hair fell on the page he blew it off and read on' (We are tempted to comment in Sam Weller's words, 'That's philosophy, sir, ain't it'?).

One reason why the Schoolmen exercised such fascination was that not only were they concerned with cases of conscience still contemporary, they adhered to the mediaeval assumption that religion was concerned with the whole of life. Nothing escaped its effects or its scrutiny. This was basic to the ministry of Herbert's country parson. One whose life was principally in other spheres, Robert Sanderson (1587–1663), chaplain to Charles I, Regius professor at Oxford and, after the Restoration, bishop of Lincoln, declared in one of his sermons:

God has made us sociable creatures, contrived us into policies, and societies, and commonwealths; made us fellow-members of one body, and *every one another's*

members. As therefore we are not born, so neither must
we live, to and for ourselves alone; but our parents, and
friends, and acquaintances, nay, every man of us hath
a kind of right and interest in every other man of us,
and our Country and the Commonwealth in us all.[12]

This, in its sentiments reminiscent of a famous passage
of John Donne, was being assailed by the triumph of
individualism, which was anticipated before the 'modern'
age in the twelfth century in reaction from the 'liturgical
state' of Charlemagne and the bleakness and cruelty of
early mediaeval life, which must never be forgotten. The
corporate and the collective can be monstrous tyranny as we
have seen in Stalinism. The 'search for the self' in Abelard,
Bernard and the later mystics, in spite of some unguarded
expressions in the last about being lost in God, led to the
discovery of 'the basic human values of friendship and self
understanding' and in Aelred of Rievaulx's phrase, that 'God
is friendship'.[13] There is individualism in the gospel itself, in
the ministry of Jesus and the testimony of St. Paul. This was
again recovered at the time of the Reformation, by Luther
above all, but it was much wider than a religious movement,
ranging from the use of glass in mirrors (many people had
not hitherto known what they looked like), the provision of
private rooms in houses, the heroic exploits of explorers to the
rise of capitalism. It embraced both catholicism and protestantism. The seventeenth century was the bridge between the
mediaeval world and that of the Enlightenment, and this had
an effect on pastoral theology and the parson's role. But the
great casuists, as Thomas Wood said, 'did not shirk the task
of indicating how Christian moral principles were intended
to operate in every sphere of human life, both private and
public'.[14]

They were bitterly opposed to the Jesuits. They would all
have agreed with the title of a publication of Richard Baxter's
in 1659, *A Key for Catholics to Open the Juggling of the
Jesuits*. Their castigations were no more severe than those of
Lettres Provinciales and Port Royal. They owed something to
sheer anti-papalism and to patriotism (vestiges of which are
mutatis mutandis still apparent among present-day English

Euro-sceptics); but chiefly they were in condemnation of the Jesuits' 'speculative laxity', their tolerance of equivocation and mental reservation, the making of things too easy for the penitent, which led to a kind of legalistic hair-splitting. Roman Catholic moral theology as a whole became juristic, strengthening those tendencies which we remarked at the very beginning and which in early centuries distinguished Roman from Celtic spirituality. The aim was not holiness, the pilgrimage to perfection, but simple minimum requirements, in the words of a Jesuit writer as recently as the early decades of this century, 'what is obligation under pain of sin; ... moral pathology'.[15]

In turn, Jeremy Taylor (1613–67), the most notable Anglican casuist, has been charged with 'pastoral cruelty'. Robert Sanderson accused him of Pelagianism, and he was against the stream and suspected by many, in that he did not accept the traditional Augustinian doctrine of original sin. This could lead to such moral rigour as was in effect salvation by works. S.T. Coleridge in the nineteenth century maintained that his writing on repentance would drive men to despair and that 'the necessary consequence of Taylor's scheme is a conscience worrying, casuistical, monkish work-holiness'. It is hard for us to recognize that so far from being grim and joyless, Augustinianism and Calvinism were liberating. They made salvation dependent on God's grace, not on our efforts. Article XVII of the Church of England declares that 'the godly consideration of Predestination and our Election in Christ, is full of sweet, pleasant and unspeakable comfort to godly persons'. Coleridge said that Calvinism is a lamb in wolf's skin, 'cruel in the phrase but not in the doctrine', 'horrible for the race, but full of consolation to the suffering individual'.[16]

Yet there is an attraction in Taylor's ascetic theology which helped to draw the young John Wesley in the next century to give all his life to God. There is severity, discipline, mortification, but these result in 'a holy and amiable captivity to the Spirit; the will of man is in love with those chains which draw us to God, and loves the fetters that confine us to the pleasures and religion of the Kingdom'. And this means that 'our light must be so shining, our conversation so exemplar, as to draw all the world after us; that they that will not, may be ashamed, and they that will, may be allured by the beauty of the flame'.[17] Taylor veers to catholic rather than the protestant theology, as Wesley did, in that love rather than faith is the key to the Christian life. He says that theology is a divine life rather than a divine knowledge, and goes on: 'In Heaven indeed we shall first see, and then love; but here on earth we must first love, and love will open our eyes as well as our hearts; and we shall then see and perceive and understand'.[18]

Taylor advocated daily communion. His doctrine is 'high' by Prayer Book standards and Herbert's. His pastoral theology is ecclesiological, beginning with the church, the pilgrim community, 'rightly and duly' gathered around Word and sacrament. 'The eucharist is the fulness of all the mysteriousness of our religion (*Clerus Domini*).' Opposed to transubstantiation, he believes that in eucharistic consecration there is 'a change of condition, of sanctification and usage' in the elements: 'They remain in substance what they were, but in relation to him are more'; They are what they were, but they are more than what they were before'.[19] Hebrews, chapter seven, influences his doctrine of the eucharistic sacrifice. Christ is a high priest continually 'and offers still the one perfect Sacrifice ... And this also his ministers do on earth. They offer up the same Sacrifice to God, the Sacrifice of the Cross by prayers, and a commemorating rite and a representment ...'. This commemorative sacrifice is taken up into Christ's heavenly intercession. There is a seriousness and a passion in sharp contrast to what Kenneth Stevenson has called the 'neo-Zwinglian chumminess' of some modern celebrations.

> We sinners thy unworthy servants, in remembrance of thy life-giving passion, thy cross and thy pains, thy death and thy burial, thy resurrection from the dead, and thy ascension into heaven, thy sitting at the right hand of God, making intercession for us, and expecting with fear and trembling ...; *do humbly present unto thee, O Lord, this present sacrifice of remembrance and thanksgiving*, humbly and passionately.[20]

The High Churchmen remained, what they always had been, a minority, though they persisted in spite of the defection of the Nonjurors. The predominate party in the English church were the 'latitude' men as their detractors called them, the moralists. But they gave pastoral guidance for daily living and robbed religion of its mystique less than has been supposed. *The Whole Duty of Man* (1657) became almost the charter of Anglican spirituality for more than a century and was instrumental in the conversion of the great Cambridge Evangelical Charles Simeon (1759–1836). It is a companion to the Prayer Book and encourages 'a godly, righteous and sober life'. There are wise counsels on preparation for communion which include meditations which encourage a penitential realism in contemplation of Christ's sufferings and death, but they do not soar to the heavenly places with Taylor. It is tempting to say that this is of more pastoral use for the average parishioner than Taylor's exalted doctrine, but that may be to concede too much to the 'down-to-earthers'. Here, though, is Oliver Goldsmith's eighteenth-century parson from 'The Deserted Village', 'passing rich on forty pounds a year', hospitable to beggars, spendthrifts and wounded soldiers.

Thus to relieve the wretched was his pride
And e'n his failings leaned to Virtue's side
But in his duty prompt at every call,
He watch'd and wept, he pray'd and felt, for all.
And, as a bird each fond endearment tries
To tempt its new fledg'd offspring to the skies,
He tried each art, reprov'd each dull delay,
Allur'd to brighter worlds, and led the way
Beside the bed where parting life was laid,
And sorrow, guilt and pain, by turns dismay'd,
The reverend champion stood. At his control
Despair and anguish fled the struggling soul;
Comfort came down the trembling wretch to raise,
And his last faltering accents whisper'd praise.

At church with meek and unaffected grace,
His looks adorned the venerable place;

Truth from his lips prevail'd with double sway,
And fools who came to scoff remained to pray.
The service pass'd around the pious man
With steady zeal each honest rustic ran;
Even children follow'd with endearing wile,
And pluck'd his gown to share the good man's smile.
His ready smile a parent's warmth express'd,
Their welfare pleas'd him and their cares distress'd;
To them his heart, his loves, his griefs were given,
But all his serious thoughts had rest in Heaven.
As some tall cliff that lifts its awful form,
Swells from the vale, and midway leaves the storm,
Though round its breast the rolling clouds are spread,
Eternal sunshine settles on its head.

The tradition of Herbert lives on, though more eighteenth-century country parsons may have been like James Woodforde, a kind and good man, who would sit up all night with a dying parishioner and preached ethical sermons, but who was in effect a minor country gentleman who enjoyed gargantuan meals. Gareth Bennett has said that 'it is difficult to believe that his parishioners can have seen him as a figure of vital religion ... he was a figure produced by a system of social subordination, and he had neither a gospel to preach nor a sacramental system which involved his people'.[21]

But the pastor is still not only the parson, but the *country* parson. It was Methodism, which Wesley, somewhat illogically, wished to remain as an order within the Church of England, which broke the parish boundaries to reach the new industrial populations. Its itinerancy and flexibility were later effective on the Western frontier, where, as Stephen Neill said, Methodist outriders were the pioneers of evangelism and the bishops followed in the train. And Methodism gave pastoral charge to the laity. The preachers were evangelists and pastors *pastorum*. Methodist pastoral work was done in bands and classes, what today would be called support groups, with some affinities with the Religious Societies of the late seventeenth and early eighteenth centuries. The rules were severe. The class-meetings were confessionals, maligned to the fury of the Roman Bishop Richard Challoner, as coveys of Roman Catholicism; but they were lay. Martin Thornton made the engaging suggestion that the Methodist class-meeting 'in part reviving the English empirical tradition would have been far more creative had Parson Woodforde presided'.[22] But this is in some ways to miss the point. The parson should not necessarily preside. He may not be there at all. There were Anglican laymen in the eighteenth century who exercised the pastoral office. Dr. Johnson, who ghosted sermons and intermittently attended the liturgy and wrote prayers, was alone with Catherine Chambers, the old companion of his family, at her dying; he prayed with her most movingly and saw her tenderly through the veil.

In the nineteenth century, however, the parson became increasingly a more than ever distinctive figure, with a more separate professional identity, trained in a theological college, wearing a uniform, distinguishable from the squire or the politician. But this is to anticipate.

Evangelicalism exalted the preacher; but it was to a large extent after the clergymen – the Grimshaws, Berridges and Newtons of the eighteenth century – a movement of wealthy layfolk, of household religion and social reform within the British constitution and the state system. There was a certain pastoral care of 'the downstairs', as there was a longing to convert the heathen at home and abroad; but the one, sometimes by a certain condescension, and the other, in spite of Christlike heroism and sacrifice, as the agents of imperialism. There was no *kenosis*. Yet we must not blame Evangelicals for lack of a ministry which has not yet been achieved except at Golgotha, or debunk the Martyns, the Wilberforces, the Shaftesburys. The clergy were above all preachers (Simeon attracted far greater crowds than Newman); pastorally there was a clerical-lay partnership. Simeon's spirituality was summed up in these words: 'The Bible first, the Prayer Book next, and all other books and doings in subordination to both.' 'The finest sight short of heaven,' he once declared, 'would be a whole congregation using the prayers of the liturgy in the spirit of them'.[23]

This is not dissimilar to the Anglican Newman, deploring strange ways in religion, pleading for the tradition: 'If (men) would but follow the Church; come together in prayer on Sundays and Saints' days, nay, every day; honour the rubric by keeping it obediently, and conforming their families to the *spirit* of the Prayer-book, I say that on the whole they would practically do vastly more good than by trying new religious plans, founding new religious societies, or striking out new religious views'.[24]

The Oxford Movement was an attempt to revive the old High Church tradition and to republish, both in literature and the life of the church, the teaching of the Caroline divines. John Keble was a country parson for most of his life, commuting from Hampshire to fulfil his duties as professor of poetry at Oxford and in the end withdrawing from academe so that he refused an invitation to preach the University sermon. He had no desire to believe or teach or do anything that would have been alien to his father — a sure sign that he was to be the passive instrument of change! He was the parson, who would bring down his cane on the shoulders of a boy who did not doff his cap to the rector. He made his sermons dull, that God might be glorified rather than the preacher praised. 'Don't be original,' he wrote to Newman who had sent him a sermon for comment. He designed the pews of his church at Hursley as prie-dieux. When the Methodist preacher from Southampton visited Hursley to see Richard Cromwell's grave and 'found' Keble, the latter was the more bashful and embarrassed and yet most cordial, offering to do anything in his power to serve the minister, who was much moved by the sheer beauty of Keble's face.

Owen Chadwick has encapsulated Keble's pastoral character:

He was always high-buttoned, with a three inch collar of self-distrust and a white tie of rare clerisy ...
Imagine a country parson, in charge of two parish churches and a chapel in a schoolroom; with a sick wife needing constant attention and in the end in a bath-chair; with a curate compelled by the bishop to be no more than a deacon for sixteen years; a country parson who reconstructed both churches

and built the schoolroom chapel; who taught in the
school for an hour every morning and more on
Sundays; who visited the sick steadily and kept his
confirmation classes for six months; who conducted
an exhausting correspondence in the guidance of souls
outside the parish; who welcomed visits from penitents
and endured visits from sightseers; who was so engaged
in the national affairs of the Church that he often
needed to run to Oxford or London to meet or protest;
who nevertheless succeeded in publishing an edition
of Hooker so excellent that it was used, with minor
revision, a century later; in writing a two-volume life
of Bishop Wilson, and printing a volume and more of
sermons, and a translation of the Psalms, and two fat
volumes in the Latin language on Homer and ancient
literature; in translating St. Irenaeus and in publishing
at least twenty-two pamphlets and several important
articles; who completed all this literary and political
activity while keeping his parishioners as his first call;
and whose single excess was in self-depreciation.[25]

Keble was *stupor mundi*, a compliment paid by James I to the
country clergy, though he did have servants, no children, no
telephone and no motor car.

In the succession of Keble was Edward King (1829–1910),
principal of Cuddesdon, Regius professor of moral and
pastoral theology at Oxford and bishop of Lincoln, where
he was put on trial on charges of ritualism. It has been said
that if canonisation were of the Anglican ethos he might be
one of those raised to the altar. The young daughter of the
present bishop of Lincoln singled out his portrait from those
of all her father's predecessors as that which most spoke to
her. As with Keble, people spoke of the beauty of holiness
shining through King's face. A shepherd visiting his chapel
and noticing the candles on the altar, then regarded as very
extreme, commented: 'I see that yours is a yon-side religion,
sir'. He was the first bishop of the post-reformation church
in England to wear a mitre. A rustic said that it looked like
a beehive on his head; out of which, added another, there
comes all honey and sweetness.

King left few literary remains, but Owen Chadwick has compared some haphazard student notes of his 1874 Oxford lectures, published by Mowbrays in 1932 under the title *Pastoral Lectures of Bishop Edward King*, with a definitive work of pastoral theology published in 1852 by J.J. Blunt, Lady Margaret professor of divinity at Cambridge and going through six editions by the time King taught. Its full title is *The Duties of the Parish Priest.*

There are similarities. King summarises Blunt and endorses him when he insists that the church is not the clergy alone. The laity must realise their membership, their obligations and their rights. They both deal with the Prayer Book order for the Visitation of the Sick and the need to use it flexibly. They both stress the value of the absolution of the sick, which had become controversial in King's time because of the Oxford Movement's revival of the practice of confession. Blunt says that it is a relief to the clergy that they are commissioned by the church to make this declaration; and that to absolve from *actual* sin is no different from the implied forgiveness of *original* sin in baptism.

King borrows Blunt's advice on how to preach and the need for study and careful preparation not to be neglected under the pressures of parish life. He also invokes Augustine and Gilbert Burnet and his French contemporary Bishop Felix Dupanloup, whom Blunt could not have known and would no more than Keble have used because he was a Roman Catholic. King is becoming less insular, more ecumenical. King says little about children or the village school, except that babies are potentially 'jewels in the crown of Christ' and affection for boys must not be lost when they become awkward and unattractive adolescents. Neither author says much about marriage or preparation for it. They recognise its sacredness. Between the two moral theologians, the first English divorce law had reached the statute book in 1857, but King merely warns his students against the salacious reading of accounts of adulteries in the newspapers. Both expect pastors to be learned and prescribe programmes of reading, with a sad lack of church history. Blunt's is more apologetic and polemical. The theology of the English

Reformation is all important for him, whereas King omits contemporary Protestant and Evangelical authors, nowhere mentions Luther or the Reformers except Calvin, whose *Institutes* should be read. And, unlike Blunt who dislikes non-Anglicans and those with an ambiguous relation to the English church, he speaks most approvingly of John Wesley. This may in part have been due to the abolition of church rates by Gladstone in 1868, so that Nonconformist anger at having to pay for the maintenance of the naves of parish churches was appeased and there was greater understanding and the possibility of friendship.

King would have his students read the notoriously lax Jesuit casuist, Hermann Busenbaum, Aquinas's *Summa Theologica* and Pascal, both the *Pensées* and the satirical *Lettres provinciales*. He insists that they read great poetry, the classics, Dante, Shakespeare, Milton and Tennyson (unlike his contemporary Dean Richard Church, he has no time for Browning); and 'good novels'. No more than Donald MacKinnon, in his inaugural lecture as Norris Hulse professor of divinity at Cambridge in 1961, does he regard these last as a waste of time: 'You will thus travel into the circumstances, conditions and situations of life'.[26] What he, who once read the work of an agnostic on his knees, though he defended *Lux Mundi*, would have thought of our modern uncensored fiction, some of it of genius and profound religious as well as human insight, I do not know; though it is never fair to pose to a figure of the past the questions of a different age.

King's pastor is to go round his parish as upon his knees. He gives an outline of contemplative methods of prayer, though no real instruction; and he advises reading of the medieval mystics. Unlike Blunt, he anticipates both the modern pastor's need to study human nature and modern trends in spirituality. There must be a rule of life, balance between the various essential activities, time for quiet and prayer and an ideal of holiness, missing from Blunt. Reverence pervades all: reverence for God in worship, reverence for all men and women as bearing the image of God. This is the contribution of the Oxford Movement to pastoral theology. Newman brought to R.W. Church a sense of 'the awfulness of things unseen'. King would have coveted this for every priest.[27]

But the Oxford Movement was not only Tractarian, as in Keble and later in King. Hurrell Froude had deplored the 'gentleman heresy,' and from the second half of the nineteenth century there was great searching of conscience because of the appalling condition of the urban poor. The establishment with its comfortable respectability, its wealth and those dreary Prayer Book services, which were one reason why Newman said he would never return to Anglicanism, had nothing to offer. So the Oxford Movement became the Anglo-Catholic revival. Its priests took over the Roman Mass, in English, introduced reservation, benediction and exposition of the blessed sacrament, sacramental confession, devotion to the Virgin, and requiems. They brought light and colour into the drab churches of the drab streets: candles and incense and holy water, ceremonies and processions and gorgeously vested priests. 'Magnify your office,' said the Anglican Newman, and they did. Priestly authority was paramount, often against bishops. Some became 'Father says' parishes. Writes Alan Wilkinson: 'Anglo-Catholic priests who, in righteous anger, swept away box pews because they divide the Body of Christ by social class, then erected screens to separate themselves and their semi-clericalized servers from laypeople in the nave'.[28]

Celibacy helped in the deprived areas of poverty and violence; and above all, the restoration of the religious life for men and women from the 1840s onwards. The Anglo-Catholic witness extended overseas, most of all, in Southern Africa, where the religious communities have been in the forefront of the struggle against apartheid, though at great emotional cost and self-sacrifice and the price of some hard lessons as they sought not simply to befriend Africans but a complete identification, hard for whites. For some, like Trevor Huddleston, the struggle for black liberation has become almost the whole of Christianity.

The First World War helped to vindicate some of the practices for which priests in the 1880s and 90s had been brought to trial and imprisoned. Amid the slaughter and the grief of bereavement, prayers for the dead became a pastoral necessity. And the priests brought a ministry which somehow transcended that of the unprepared officer caste, though not all were without jingoism.

At home and out of church they ran dances like Father Robert Dolling in Portsmouth, the priests protected by their cassocks. They did not eschew drinking and smoking – 'gin and lace' characterise some of their successors to this day – and hated some aspects of the Nonconformist conscience, though they were often rigorous on contraception, abortion and divorce. They ignored and despised the Free Churches, concerned only with rapprochement with Rome, though there were some deep personal friendships between priests and ministers and sometimes the Free Churchmen found them easier than starchy Broad Churchmen or fundamentalist Evangelicals. Their heyday was between the wars. Like all churches in England they began the peace of 1945 with overwhelming confidence, unconscious that they were at the beginning of their decline. It is not easy to assess their effectiveness, or whether they do not represent a temporary mutation of Christianity. In spite of their belief in the *opus operatum* nature of priesthood, it was often the personality of the priest which won souls.

Something of their greatest power and passion is seen in the addresses of Bishop Frank Weston of Zanzibar, an extremist, scholarly advocate of kenotic christology, to the Anglo-Catholic Congress of 1923. He preached Jesus, one and the same Jesus, on the throne of his glory, in the blessed sacrament, received in communion, mystically present in prayer and enthroned in the hearts and bodies of his brothers and sisters up and down the country. 'It is folly,' he admonished – 'it is madness – to suppose that you can worship Jesus in the sacraments and Jesus on the Throne of glory, when you are sweating him in the souls and bodies of His children.'

You have got your Mass, you have got your Altar, you have begun to get your Tabernacle. Now go out into the highways and hedges ... Go out and look for Jesus in the ragged, in the naked, in the oppressed and sweated, in those who have lost hope, in those who are struggling to make good. Look for Jesus. And when you see him, gird yourselves with his towel and try to wash their feet.[29]

It remains first to try to discern amid all the changes, developments and divisions what we may conclude about the Anglican pastoral tradition; and then to confront it with some of the particular questions of our time.

It must be admitted that the Anglican pastoral ministry owes much to the privileged and legally safeguarded position of the parochial clergy in England. Yet the principle that their ministry is for all, whether churchgoers or not is truly of the gospel. It is made more difficult in multi-faith societies where Christians may be a minority or a small majority, where the parochial system has broken down into pluralities and the pastor becomes in effect a 'Mass priest', but it still applies. No one is outside this ministry. The priest himself – and I use the masculine because that is how it has been – must, as Charles Smyth used to summarise it, say his prayers, read his Bible and love his people. And this with 'undistinguishing regard' – a phrase of Charles Wesley's – and complete impartiality. He will intercede for them daily and offer his own soul for theirs. He is girt about with the liturgy and offices. He will preside at worship and see the eucharist as the centre of the church's life from which all else flows. He will not hesitate, as a forgiven sinner himself, 'to declare and pronounce to (Christ's) people being penitent, the absolution and remission of their sins'. He will be a preacher to proclaim the good news of God even in the worst circumstances, to offer Christ before he makes demands, and to inflame human hearts with the divine love. And this out of a sensitive knowledge of 'what is in' human beings. He knows he has to stand before people in Christ's stead. He will teach, expounding the Scriptures and the creeds, relating faith to life, trying to resolve cases of conscience, and helping people to pray. He will not be doctrinaire or self-assured. He will be honest about his doubts and struggles and not always afraid, though this is not in the Anglican tradition, to share his own experiences as did Paul. He will seek a holy people and leave no doubt that he himself is a pilgrim of holiness.

Beyond all pastoral care his aim will be to bring people to union with God in Christ and to a life beyond the things of time and to find their place in the story of Jesus, his finished and continuing work.

Much of that, I hope, still applies and suggests that the pastoral vocation may not have in essence much altered. But there are problems peculiar to our time.

What of the Bible? What is its authority today? Do we read long passages in public such as turned the Prayer Book Offices into services of the Word? Do we, with Evangelicals, have our daily portion, not confined to our own favourite passages? Do we take the traditional catholic view that the church must interpret Scripture in accordance with rigid orthodoxy and not let the Word go free, which sometimes means casualties, though at less risk of dogmatic and obscurantist imprisonment unless we are fundamentalists. What of criticism? Is there a 'spiritual' reading innocent of Bultmann, Nineham, Knox and Sanders, who should be exiled from the place of prayer and who have made some innocent souls cry with the Magdalene at the tomb, 'They have taken away my Lord and I know not where they have laid him'? I think the scholars I have mentioned show the necessity of faith rather than being destructive of it. The pastor cannot work without the Scriptures, the foundation documents of Christianity, and must bring to their study all the resources of scholarship. If you believe that they are the witnesses to those events and that history which is decisive for the whole cosmos, you cannot know too much about them. It is important to recognise, however, that their 'strangeness' is not, *pace* Dennis Nineham, so much due to the great cultural divide or to a different view of the Universe, as to their revolutionary revaluation of our natural norms, and that they may unfold their deepest secrets to many an untutored soul, innocent of scholarship, who loves God and neighbour.

And is there not an identity crisis in the ministry? This is due in part to shortage of clergy, but also to the reaffirmation of the laity, the insistence of the liturgical movement that it is the whole people of God who are celebrants of the eucharist and not the priests alone and that there must be lay participation. I remember Ronald Jasper saying that the priest is more the producer of the liturgy than the leading actor. There is also charismatic renewal, with its stress on the diversity of the Spirit's gifts and on 'every member ministry'.[30]

There is also secularisation and the fear and mistrust of religion and its all-embracing claims, its official representatives, and its bad and oppressive record in many ways. Death is no longer all-pervasive in the West and North. There is more fear of dying and this may be overcome by pain-killing drugs or, some would urge, voluntary euthanasia. The priest is not needed at the death-bed. The subvenite is outmoded. And so much is now done by social services and other agencies. Are we not blundering amateurs, our role usurped by psychologists, disciples of Freud or Jung? In many realms, in church and out, the pastor is no longer the parson, the persona of the community.

There was a lecture given recently in Oxford by a Dominican on Jung, his types and archetypes and particularly issues of gender. He offered all this brilliantly for an hour and a quarter as a way of human understanding, if not in some sense of salvation. Afterwards a member of the audience commented critically that no one would have known from anything he said that he was a priest, or even a Christian, though he wore his white habit. He rejoined that he was using modern approaches and discoveries ultimately in the service of Christ. He presided at Mass with great conviction and humanity very different from the expressionless race track rapidity of a Benedictine the year before.

It is in the realms of bio-ethics and sexuality that there are peculiar problems of acute casuistry. What about experimentation, *in vitro* fertilization, abortion of the handicapped and so much else, even the possibility of the creation of life? Fortunately moral theologians are engaged in these matters and a book such as the Methodist Stanley Hauerwas's *Suffering Presence* is wise and good. But there is also the belief that what we interpret in moral categories may be physiological more than psychological, much less ethical. I know a fine and compassionate neuro-psychiatrist whose moral philosophy is that of Hamlet, 'There's nothing good or bad but thinking makes it so.'

Sexuality is now no longer a subject only to be whispered. Sexual orientation may be spoken of freely. We are no longer afraid to admit that some of the finest pastors and many Anglo-Catholic priests – more so than Romans – have been homosexuals.[31] We do not share the inhibitions of those who balked at the completion of the larger than life statue of Edward King in Lincoln Cathedral, which shows him with hands outstretched in confirmation or blessing, but lacks the child on whom those hands were to be laid for fear of sexual implications. Admittedly greater openness and honesty sometimes leads to distressing adolescent doubts as to sexuality. We now recognize that Jesus himself, if he were truly human, could not have been immune from sexuality, and that the woman in Simon the Pharisee's house who anointed his feet and wiped them with her hair was performing an erotic act which he did not repudiate but saw as the transmutation of her sexuality into the love of a forgiving Lord. 'A man and a woman discussing God together in an emotionally charged atmosphere will be deceiving themselves if they think this is a straightforwardly spiritual or pastoral encounter' – so Rowan Williams on Teresa of Avila and her strong attachment as a young nun to an older priest. And although a greater freedom and naturalness in man-woman relationships may be wondrously liberating and consoling, there are obvious dangers and nature takes a terrible revenge on promiscuity. Yet, I would assert that the sexual impulse is not itself the root of sin, and that human desire, though so often debased into lust, is a God given hunger for his love. The people many Christians would canonise today, like Martin Luther King and Nelson Mandela, have been heroic and suffering fighters against injustice, but not necessarily conforming to the strictest rules of sexual behaviour.

There is also the change in marriage mores, of couples cohabiting before a marriage contract either civil or religious, and of the increase of divorce, not least among the clergy, with frequent damage to children. And what of single parent families? Some deserve deepest sympathy, some indeed represent triumphs of grace, but in spite of some feminists they cannot be condoned as the norm. Meanwhile our Lord's attitude to the family in all the gospels is disturbing to conventional Christian teaching, if studied in its full implications, though doubtless conditioned by the eschatological demands of his mission. And there is the whole change in the position of women in society and the bitter controversy as to whether this means that they should be priests in addition to being pastors and preachers. I do not think that this can forever be denied in a world in which women are admitted to the most prestigious positions – not even in Rome or the Eastern Church where, I am told, some Anglican converts are agitating for it. I recognise that it will cause great changes even in the nature of priesthood as understood in the more rigid catholicism. Those who fear that it will revolutionise the whole concept of ministry in the church are not fighting phantoms. And there is that in extreme feminism which indeed makes us tremble for the Ark of God.

These are matters which to rehearse is to come under the criticism of being trite. The world is writing the agenda and, while I believe that for the church the Incarnation should do that, it is not easy for those who believe in the Word made flesh to resist the social tides without becoming eccentric and sectarian and appearing as strange as the seventeenth-century Quakers, the nineteenth-century Mormons, or the twentieth-century Jehovah's Witnesses. We must live our lives and exercise our ministries before God, which means that there must always and everywhere be compassion and not rigorism or legalism and yet no countenancing of such uncharted freedom as itself leads to slavery or the destruction of human life and its relationships. Sometimes we have to be against the stream, though we be persecuted and ostracised. There is a letter to *The Guardian* newspaper in the United Kingdom, dated September 21st 1992, in which Bishop Rowan Williams sees the British financial disasters as giving the game away about 'markets'; 'they are after all, only the masks of old fashioned greed and moral tone-deafness'. They have come near to destroying the Third World with a harvest of wrath still to be reaped. We have kept hungry and greedy guard dogs and not been too concerned when they have savaged the neighbours' children; but now they begin to turn on our own. This will be debated, and divisive.

There are those who would say that a Christian economics is no more possible than a Christian mathematics. Others claim that in a fallen world 'the Market' may be more merciful than socialism. It is not easy to be both pastoral and prophetic, to be ministers of reconciliation and contenders for justice, fighters for the oppressed, to combine Christ's woes on the rich with his accepting of their hospitality and clear desire to save. To relate religion to the whole life, which was the ministry of our forbears, becomes ever more complex. Have we the knowledge? Does the gospel itself provide for a world 2000 years on, which it was thought would not long survive Jesus Christ and his judgement? We have to decide in the company of our fellow Christians and in the light of the Holy Tradition and of what seems to be God's will for us, what are the last ditch issues, where indeed we ought to be *mutatis mutandis* with John Keble who said, 'If the Church of England were to fail it should be found in my parish' (We would say 'the Church and Gospel of Christ'). Owen Chadwick has remarked that it takes a moment to see 'how cloud-capped are the towers thus defended'.[32]

There is poetry in the pastoral heart, perhaps more than prophecy. Yet David Gascoyne spoke of One who is 'the Christ of Revolution and of Poetry'. But above all is that solemn obligation which the Prayer Book Ordinal enjoins:

Have always therefore printed in your remembrance, how great a treasure is committed to your charge. For they are the sheep of Christ whom he bought with his death and for whom he shed his blood.

Notes

1. For Theodore see Charles Smyth, *The Genius of the Church of England* (London: SPCK, 1947), 29, 53 n. 24; and also, John T. McNeill and Helena M. Gamer, *Medieval Handbooks of Penance* (New York: Columbia University Press, 1938).
2. *Saepius Officio: The Reply of the English Archbishops to the Bull Apostolical Curae of Pope Leo XIII Concerning Anglican Ordinations to all the Bishops of The Catholic Church in the Year 1897* (London: 1897), 37.

3. *cf.* Basil Hall, *Humanists and Protestants: 1500–1900* (Edinburgh: T & T Clark, 1990), 237–54; Patrick Collinson, *The Elizabethan Puritan Movement* (Berkeley: University of California Press, 1967).

4. Henry R. McAdoo, *The Structures of Caroline Moral Theology* (London: Longmans, Green & Co., 1949).

5. Quoted in J.T. Wilkinson, ed., *The Reformed Pastor* (London: Longmans, Green & Co., 1949).

6. Quoted in Gordon S. Wakefield, *Puritan Devotion: Its Place in the Development of Christian Piety* (London: Epworth Press, 1957), 154.

7. The term 'Anglican' was unknown at the time, possibly invented by Newman in the 19th century and used by F.D. Maurice and Charles Kingsley; *The Oxford English Dictionary*, though, has an entry for 1797. See J.R. Wright, 'Anglicanism, *Ecclesia Anglicana*, and Anglican: An Essay on Terminology,' in *The Study of Anglicanism*, ed. Stephen Sykes and John Booty (London: SPCK, 1988), 424–29.

8. Richard Strier, *Love Unknown: Theology and Experience in George Herbert's Poetry* (Chicago: University of Chicago Press, 1983), vx.

9. Owen C. Watkins, *The Puritan Experience* (London: Routledge and K. Paul, 1972), 211; see also Chana Bloch, *Spelling The Word: George Herbert and The Bible* (Berkeley: University of California Press 1985).

10. McAdoo, 8,12.

11. Herbert does not talk of 'celebration', a term which the Cambridge scholar F.J.A. Hort two hundred years later disliked because of its Roman associations.

12. Robert Sanderson, 'Sermon IV: Ad Populum,' in *Works*, ed., W. Jackson (Oxford: University Press, 1854), 3:101–02.

13. See Colin Morris, *The Discovery of the Individual, 1050–1200* (London: SPCK, 1972).

14. Thomas Wood, *English Casuistical Divinity During the Seventeenth Century: With Special Reference to Jeremy Taylor* (London: SPCK, 1952), 58.

15. Preface to T. Slater, *A Manual of Moral Theology for English-Speaking Countries*, 6th ed. (1928); quoted in Wood, 65 n. 1, to whose treatment I am much indebted.

16. S.T. Coleridge, *Notes on English Divines*, ed. Derwent Coleridge (London: E. Moxon, 1853), 2:38; *cf* C. Fitzsimmons Allison, 'The Pastoral Cruelty of Jeremy Taylor's Theology,' *The Modern Churchman*, 15 (January 1972): 123–31; also, Margaret R. Miles, *The Image and Practice of Holiness* (London: SCM, 1989), 170*ff*.

17. J. Taylor, 'Sermon I: Of the Spirit of Grace,' in *Works*, ed. C.P. Eden (London: Rivington, 1848), 4:335; 'Sermon X: The Minister's duty in Life and Doctrine,' in *Works* (London, 1850), 8:502.

18. Taylor, 'Sermon VI: Via Intelligentiàe,' in *Works*, 8:368.
19. McAdoo, *The Eucharistic Theology of Jeremy Taylor Today* (Norwich: Canterbury Press, 1968), 41, 139*ff*.
20. Kenneth Stevenson, *Eucharist and Offering* (New York: Pueblo, 1986), 158.
21. Gareth Bennett, *To the Church of England: Essays and Papers*, ed. Geoffrey Rowell (Worthing, England: Churchman's Publishing, 1988), 118*ff*.
22. Martin Thornton, *English Spirituality: An Outline of Ascetical Theology According to the English Pastoral Tradition* (London: SPCK, 1963), 285. For Woodforde see various editions of his *Diary of a Country Parson*, notably from Oxford University Press edited by J. Beresford in five volumes (1924–31), and no. 514 in the World's Classics Series.
23. Charles Smyth, *Simeon and Church Order: A Study of the Origins of the Evangelical Revival in Cambridge in the Eighteenth Century* (Cambridge: University Press, 1940), 291.
24. J.H. Newman, 'Sermon XII: Profession Without Ostentation,' in *Parochial and Plain Sermons* (London: Rivingtons, 1887), 1:154.
25. Owen Chadwick, *The Spirit of the Oxford Movement: Tractarian Essays* (Cambridge: University Press, 1990), 56, 58–59.
26. *cf.* Donald MacKinnon, *Borderlands of Theology and Other Essays*, ed. G.W. Roberts and D.E. Smucker (Lutterworth Press, 1968), 51.
27. Chadwick, 289–306.
28. Alan Wilkinson, *The Community of the Resurrection: A Centenary History* (London: SCM Press, 1992), 98.
29. Frank Weston, 'Our Present Duty,' in *Report of the Anglo-Catholic Congress, Subject: The Gospel of God* (London: Society of SS. Peter and Paul, 1923), 185–86.
30. *cf.* Paul Bradshaw, 'Patterns of Ministry,' in *Studia Liturgica*, 15 (1982/1983): 49–64.
31. W.S.F. Pickering, *Anglo-Catholicism: A Study in Religious Ambiguity* (London: Routledge, 1989), 184–206.
32. Chadwick, 62.

Anglicanism
and the Visual Arts

In the service of the church Keble caused the visual arts to be employed as well as deploying his own literary gifts. The present aspect of the parish church of Hursley and its stained glass owes much to the vicar at the time of the Victorian alterations. Keble thus devoted himself to choosing architect and stained glass artist and to the theological and practical considerations involved in the work. In this, like many an incumbent who sets in train alterations to the fabric of a church, he was to influence the ambience of worship for generations to come. However the readership of *The Christian Year* may fluctuate, the daylight unfalteringly illuminates the designs Keble chose in the building he ordered.

Keble's concern with the visual arts was in the first place to find an architect for the development of the church at Hursley. Funded by the proceeds from Keble's literary achievements this work was given in 1846 to J.P. Harrison, who was to be also responsible for the lych gate, schools and schoolmaster's house. In the same county, of Hampshire, he also designed St. John's, Purbrook, in 1843, and St. Matthew's, Netley Marsh, in 1855.

Tom Mozley assessed Keble's architectural interests coolly: 'Newman never went into architecture ... Froude was most deeply interested in architecture, but it is plain that he was more penetrated and inspired by St. Peter's than ever by Cologne Cathedral ... Keble was a latitudinarian if not a utilitarian, in architecture.'[1] James F. White concludes that whereas gothic kindled a religious crusade in the Cambridge Camden Society, at Oxford by contrast the ecclesiological study of this period of architecture was more of an antiquarian pastime.[2]

It is with the programme of the stained glass windows and the artists in his circle that Keble is to be seen engaging fully. Two influences will have worked on him powerfully. The first is the parish church of St. Mary the Virgin, Fairford, Gloucestershire, remembered since his childhood there for its twenty-eight late fifteenth-century windows depicting scenes from Eden to the Last Judgement. The second is the publication in 1843 of *The Symbolism of Churches and Church Ornaments: A Translation of the First Book of the Rationale Divinorum Officiorum, written by William Durandus*, the thirteenth century bishop of Mende. Translated and edited with a lengthy introductory essay by the two prolific founder members of the Cambridge Camden Society, Benjamin Webb and John Mason Neale, this book guided generations of church builders and the artists and craftsmen whom they employed.[3]

Keble's acquaintance with artists is recorded. He employed William Wailes (who had worked with Augustus Pugin) to execute the windows for Hursley, but not without William Butterfield (whose fully developed personal styling of All Saints, Margaret Street, London was not to erupt until 1849) having prepared the scheme.[4] This intervention of Butterfield's reversed an initiative of Keble's with three artists in his circle, but it has to be remembered that Butterfield was virtually court architect to the Cambridge Camden movement, and his advice commanded obedience.

A quieter glimpse of Keble's own taste may be gained from the three artists mentioned. Eldest was Anthony Vandyke Copley Fielding (1787–1855), a traditional landscape painter who had studied with John Varley, and who served as president of the Old Water Colour Society, much sought after as a teacher. William Dyce (1806–1864) was of a much more dynamic cast of mind: two visits to Italy and contact with the German Nazarenes (whose Christian primitivism he tried to acclimatise in Scotland) were decisively influential in his development. A successful portrait painter, he extended his range with his cartoons for the wall-paintings in the new Palace of Westminster (*Religion: Vision of Sir Galahad* and *The Baptism of Ethelbert*), and the decorations for All Saints, Margaret Street. He was appointed director of the Government School of Design in 1840 (following a tour of state schools in France, Prussia and Bavaria). George

Richmond (1809–1896) acknowledged 'gentle, visionary Blake' among the influences of his youth, and friendship with Samuel Palmer grew into a two years period spent in Rome together. In later life he was to become a fashionable portrait painter. The archbishop of Canterbury, Charles Thomas Longley, and Keble each sat to him, and the results were exhibited at the Royal Academy Exhibitions of 1863 and 1864 respectively.

Keble's commissioning of artworks prompts enquiry as to the Church of England's outlook on the visual arts. In the following pages some observations about artworks placed in churches lead on to a brief glance at Anglican writers' remarks on art. A short historical review of certain artworks in England and in the United States leads into a more detailed examination of what is proposed as being an exemplary church commission of our own century.

Artworks placed in church buildings belong, like the buildings themselves, to the people of the church.[5] The painting, the sculpting, the building is generally done by lay persons. Lay persons are generally responsible for the provision, maintenance, and, if necessary, repair, alterations or removal. It is not so with Scripture and doctrine: it has been clerics who decided the canon and who voted in the great councils. And even if we consider the giant part played by Constantine, the unbaptised layman, in the early councils, we remember too the effect of his interventions, to make the bishops of Rome more prominent than any other figure lay or ecclesiastical in the West.

Artworks by contrast appertain to the people. They belong to them as a possession and as a right; they need to be appropriate to them; they engage with them. The other side of the coin is that in most churches the clerics with their generally cerebral, conceptual and wordy formation have more often than not been related to artworks only in a negative sense, in disinterest, suspicion, distrust, antagonism, even fear. The church has in the end, even if by default, given art its autonomy. The commissioning of a great artwork is rare. One of the greatest of our century I propose to recall shortly.

Before I do so, however, it is helpful to note what the

Council of Trent had to say about art, for two reasons: (1) Trent reviewed previous decisions about art; and (2) the bulk of Anglican writers concede most of Trent's findings.[6] Absent of course in England were the twin engines of the Society of Jesus and the Inquisition to enforce obedience to central authority in artistic as in other matters.

The 1563 decree of the Council of Trent on the invoking and venerating of images of the saints affirms that images are indeed to be retained and that due honour and veneration be paid them, but it insists on careful supervision of images, recommending their explanation through preaching. Honour paid to images passes to their prototypes.

England in the same year saw the publication of the 'Homily on the Peril of Idolatry,' which flatly denounced all images. The contrary view was found in William Laud (1573–1645), Herbert Thorndike (1598–1672) and Richard Crakanthorpe (1567–1624); Laud himself, when charged at his trial with abuses in the Universities, especially Oxford, championing 'Images countenanced there by me, in diverse chapels'.

In 1684 the Court of Arches, in the case of *Cook and Others v. Tallent*, ruled in favour of the lawfulness of pictures provided they were not used for superstitious or idolatrous purposes, and this view was to prevail generally.'[7] G.W.O. Addleshaw and Frederick Etchells note the theological and liturgical tact with which the eighteenth century altar piece, with a few exceptions, 'does not overshadow the altar or attempt to rival it like so many late Gothic and baroque structures. The reredos remains secondary and the chief object in the altar place is the altar itself, to which the reredos calls attention'.[8]

This development of a continuing welcome being accorded to images, but not without their careful design and placing, is enshrined in the faculty jurisdiction. 'The task of the ecclesiastical courts in exercising the faculty jurisdiction is to ensure that the sacred uses are protected, that the parishioners are duly consulted, that the wider aesthetic interests of the public are considered, but remembering always that a parish church is a place of worship and not a museum'.[9] In this way clericalism in the choice of art for the church is held at bay, and the artist's own contribution is not unduly inhibited.

Recovery after the suppression of artworks, however, was necessarily slow. 'And Art made tongue-tied by Authority'[10] was to take time to find a voice again in the Anglican Church following the Reformation. Music instead took up the strain, and in those early Anglican days beauty was heard and not seen. In later times many a fine organ case (in itself a conspicuous and almost self-consciously eirenic item of furniture) was seen to hold apart the warring altar and pulpit. From the time of its completion (until the nineteenth century), St. Paul's Cathedral in London had the organ case carved by Grinling Gibbons in full prominence across and above the entrance to the choir.

While artworks of sacred subjects were to be found in a domestic setting, there were few in churches. So the Earl of Leicester possessed such works as *Christ calling Peter* and *John the Baptist preaching*, and a painting of 1570 shows Heaven and a human soul ascending to it past a multitude of moral perils.[11] In churches, however, a 'decent plainness' reigned, rendering the church muralist redundant; he had to scrounge for domestic religious commissions, but these would go to foreigners by choice and if funds allowed. The domestic and the ecclesiastical alone met in funeral monuments, as in West Hampnett Church where Richard Sackville's tomb (*c*.1540) has a representation of the Trinity with a naked Son reclining lifeless on his Father's arms.

By the start of the seventeenth century, it was not the ecclesiastical authorities choosing the art but the Renaissance-educated, amateur virtuosi; these were Anglicans, and they limited themselves to the less extreme aspects of catholic art. These were gentlemen addressing gentlemen, not dedicated servants of Christ proselytising among all men. Charles I was the culmination of this phase: to him as patron Rubens and Le Sueur looked, and there was a fondness for New Testament subjects. Members of the Caroline court commissioned religious subjects from Van Dyck, but none have survived. The second half of the seventeenth century is chiefly presided over, where the visual arts are concerned, by architecture and by Wren. The political compromise of

St. Paul's Cathedral as finally built opened the way for the painting of the dome spaces by James Thornhill, which he began in 1715.

This slow start to the history of Anglicanism and the visual arts is not an ecclesiastical matter only. Let Wren explain: ' ... our English Artists are dull enough at Inventions but once a foreign pattern is set, they imitate so well that commonly they exceed the original ... this shows that our natives want not a *genius* but *education* in that which is the foundation of all Mechanick Arts, a practice in designing or drawing, to which everybody in Italy, France and the Low Countries pretends to more or less'. Wren's advice was heeded and some beginnings of art education followed his strictures.

It was the native of another country who in the eighteenth century had the insight to go with the grain of the English temperament in religion. This temperament was not violently Puritan, but a puritan residue was lodged in the corner of the eye, and a suspicion of the eye's pleasure had resulted. Even Sir Thomas More had held that churches should be dark so that men's thoughts should not be distracted from their devotions, and in his *Utopia* art is no aid to worship. The other country was, of course, the United States, and Benjamin West the artist, destined to become the second president of the Royal Academy of Arts in London, succeeding Joshua Reynolds in 1792. Born in Pennsylvania in 1738 into a Quaker ethos, West came into the learned and cultured circle of the Anglican priest William Smith, who was the founding provost of what was to become the University of Pennsylvania. Arriving in England West quickly and productively entered the company and confidence of senior bishops and of the King. John Dillenberger's work on Benjamin West's many paintings with religious subject matter deserves to be better known, for West's ability to be at the head of fashion in the successive neo-Classical and proto-Romantic periods encouraged the visual arts considerably in the Church of England and not least in royal circles with the projected series on *The Progress of Revelation.*[12]

By the time of his arrival in London in 1763, West was more suave than at the start of his preceding three years in

Rome. There the blind Cardinal Albani, pleased to have as visitor this handsome Pennsylvanian, brought up, as it was put about, 'among the wigwams of the Indians', was nevertheless disturbed to hear West's exclamation before the *Apollo Belvedere*: 'My God, how like it is to a Mohawk warrior!' West went on to describe the character and activities of the young Mohawks, their dexterity with bow and arrow, elasticity of limb and expanded chests, until the Cardinal did eventually allow that 'a better criticism had rarely been passed on the statue's merits.'

The Episcopal Church record in relation to American nineteenth century artists may be studied. Did the Episcopal Church engage with such religious artists as the Anglican Thomas Cole, the Roman Catholic-patronised William Rimmer and John La Farge, the agnostic Thomas Eakins, the devout, now voguish, much forged Albert Pinkham Ryder, Elihu Vedder who was later to be absorbed into Buddhism and theosophy, the 'painterly' Robert Loftin Newman and with John Singer Sargent and Edwin Austin Abbey (Abbey painted the reredos for the Episcopal Church in Paris, France)?[13] Coming from an English writer the question is something of a taunt, yet England had not done well either, generally failing to engage creatively with artists.

Now I move to the present century and the one artwork I choose to deal with in depth. In doing so I claim greatness for it and a certain pride in the Anglican factor of the commissioning process which I hold out as a model of its kind. It may also be considered as an object lesson for future commissions in Anglicanism in other churches. The work (Plate 1) is Henry Moore's (1898–1986) *Madonna and Child* (1943–44, Hornton stone, height 59 inches) for St. Matthew's church, Northampton, in the diocese of Peterborough. The sculpture was to be a thank offering for the first fifty years of the parish. The parish was not a prestige parish, not smart, not a 'plum', but a focus nevertheless of the quiet, faithful, catholic ministry of the Church of England. A certain Bohemian chic descended on the town with the wartime relocation there of some of London's art colleges at a venue not far from St. Matthew's. The vicar was a graduate of

Keble College, Oxford, Walter Hussey (1909–1985).[14] For all the arts he had an eye, an ear, but no formal or academic formation in art. As a parish priest he was convinced that if the arts were to be any part of the worship then they needed to be of the best.

Hussey took trouble to make and to keep himself aware of the art scene. Moore's work he had seen in 1942: the air raid shelter drawings which recorded the eerie scene of Londoners retreating from the almost nightly aerial bombardment of the city's streets into the silent safety of its deserted night-time subway stations. The public found a kind of heroic stoicism in these scenes, and Hussey remembered their dignity, their power. Their author was a respected but as yet far from popularly acclaimed sculptor some eleven years his senior.[15]

The two men met for supper in a hotel. 'Would Moore do a sculpture for the church?' enquired the fastidious aesthete priest. Moore, with the North country directness that fame was never to relieve him of, expressed dislike of commissions: 'they mean stopping work on whatever else you are doing at the time'. The vicar, who was to become known as an indomitable persuader, persisted: 'if it were a Madonna and Child would you *believe* in it?' And here is Moore's reply:

Yes, I would. Though whether or not I should agree with your theology, I just do not know. *I think it is only through our art that we artists can come to understand your theology.*

This claim provides the means by which Moore's three sculptures now housed in Anglican churches may be appreciated and their line of development sought. It does more: it makes clear that theologians can only come to understand and know the artist's mode of creativity by spending time in conversation with artists.

In speaking of 'our art', Moore was surely alluding both to his own process of working and also to the world's community of sculpture of which his voracious studies had made him freeman.

Of the process of working, the engaging with chance and material, Moore thought it in general a mistake for a sculptor or painter to speak or write very often, for the characteristic reason that 'it releases tension needed for his work'. Nevertheless 'it is likely that a sculptor can give from his own conscious experience clues which will help others in their approach to sculpture'. Note *conscious*: Moore was not given to psychoanalysing.

And how has the Northampton *Madonna and Child* been received? There were vehement criticisms made in purple ink ('Maddona with Elephantiasis', 'An Insult to God', etcetera) to the newspapers. There was the intemperate outburst at the Royal Academy's Banquet of 1949 from its president, Sir Alfred Munnings, who used the BBC radio broadcast of the occasion to play to the gallery.

The all-important *people* of the parish, represented by their elected churchwardens and church council, had been given proper opportunity to meet the artist, to study maquettes, and freely to choose among them. Hussey knew the work was to be theirs: he did not manipulate them. Loyalty to a substantially modern work in their own parish church should not be a mere servile response to an overbearing parish priest. I emphasise this point as enshrining the ancient role of artworks in church as appertaining to the people.

As sometimes happens in religion, the most weighty criticism of this new religious work came from a humanist quarter and was first expressed in a lecture at the Museum of Modern Art in New York on the occasion of the 1953 Rouault exhibition.[16] Edgar Wind, then professor of philosophy and art at Smith College and shortly to become the first professor of the history of art at the University of Oxford, found our sculpture 'embarrassing to the spectators who are addressed directly and invited to participate in a ritual with which they are out of sympathy'. Wind carefully analyses the contradiction set up by the statue's upper and lower parts: these seem to be addressed, he claims, to different sensibilities, the self-conscious and fussy upper part with the rusticity of the woman's features and the child's gazing expression being aimed at a more conventional Nazarene taste (he notes the Virgin's collar and the folds of her sleeves), whereas the forceful modelling of feet and knees and the sweep of the skirt address a different viewer. He finds here the tact of compromise, but asks whether this image will bring us to our knees. This last question harks back to Wind's starting point, namely Hegel's pessimism about religious art: 'no matter how nobly and perfectly portrayed God the Father, Christ and Mary seem to be, it is no use; we no longer bend our knees before them'. This rigorous humanist approach is a salutary one for all those involved with religious and sacred art to ponder.

We can, however, go on to ask whether in this work Moore is not deploying theological thinking quite as much as tactful compromise. We have his own self-questioning during the months when he was debating whether or not to accept the commission: 'I began thinking of the *Madonna and Child* for St. Matthew's by considering in what ways a *Madonna and Child* differs from a carving of just a Mother and Child, that is, by considering how in my opinion religious art differs from secular art ... In general terms the *Madonna and Child* should have an austerity and a nobility and some touch of grandeur (even hieratic aloofness) which is missing in the everyday mother and child idea'. Moore went on to write of the subject's quiet dignity and gentleness, its sense of complete easiness and respose, adding the Stanley Spencerish reflection 'as though the Madonna could stay in that position for ever (as being in stone, she will have to do)'. The critical question of the scale of the figures (they are in fact slightly over life-size) was settled in accordance not only with the large size of the church but also with 'the human feeling I wish to express'.[17] In other words Moore's sculpture is the result of his wrestling with the age-old questions of christology, an activity which drew on his great learning about art, but not in such a way as simply to reproduce an old solution. Indeed, Wind's very diagnosis of a contradiction in this image is a pointer towards the success in Moore's attempt to depict the Theotokos and her God child. Had it not been this kind of other-worldliness in the figures of the deep-buried, down to earth shelter figures that had led Hussey in the first place to look at their creator for a new religious image?

The commissioning task was not complete, however, when the statue was manoeuvred into the church. Hussey knew that in the preliminary stages the people of the church had their part to play, and the church council they elected took their place in the process alongside their vicar. The presenting of the work to a wider public beyond the walls of the building and the boundaries both of the parish and of the town, and its reception were of concern to Hussey. We see him engaging in a careful and thorough publicising and educational exercise. The care he took at this stage is worth studying. It provides an object lesson for any church employing an artist of great merit.

Hussey enlisted at least three champions. He was accustomed as an Anglican priest to see his ministry not as limited to people of a particular education, class or age. And his three champions are, we find, aged 60, 50 and 40: an ecclesiastic, and art expert, and art publicist.

The ecclesiastic is George Bell, bishop of Chichester from 1929–1957.[18] The son of a vicar, a chaplain to and biographer of Archbishop Randall Davidson, and later a dean of Canterbury, Bell's life was spent near the centre of Anglican affairs. The only Anglican bishop of his time to have a first hand and continuing knowledge of the church in Germany, he is most largely remembered for his grasp of European politics (and it is a British Member of Parliament who is at present writing a new biography of him). He was, however, also a big mover on the ecumenical scene.

His interest in the arts was not a holiday from these primary concerns; Hussey was enlisting the support of a learned, cultured theologian and cleric for whom the arts were the flowers of the very peace for which the Second World War was being waged. And Bell's pastoral concern for the stream of artists who fled from Hitler's Germany, and for their employment, was grounded in the belief that a fight for civilization should not neglect the arts. The Bell papers in Lambeth Palace Library document the care the statesman bishop took with individual friendships: with Hans Feibusch, for instance, he entered into the practicalities of the various commissions he helped put in his way, but we hear him entering also into the exile's troubled state of mind, and then choosing a priest to help Feibusch prepare for baptism. At the time of the Henry Moore commission Bell was sixty years of age. Writing earlier in the war, Bell took as a starting point Christopher Dawson's *The Making of Europe* with its insight into mediaeval peace-society (the church) and war-society (the feudal nobility and their following). Bell saw a reassociation of the church and the artist as the factor enabling religion in its deepest sense to become once more the most potent of all influences in the regeneration of society. He proceeds to list his own 'reassociating' efforts at Canterbury as dean of the cathedral (1924–1929), and to outline practical ways in which even in wartime such developments were taking place. He concludes by quoting the second half of chorus ix from T.S. Eliot's *The Rock*.[19]

A broadcast talk thirteen years later finds Bell still looking towards Europe, still urgent for the artist. He recalls Paul Claudel's remark about the church having lost the envelope of art and resembling a man stripped of his clothes: the artist needs trusting, encouraging, helping – 'once the artist has been chosen the Church should give him freedom in the exercise of his art'.[20]

Ten years Bell's junior, Eric Newton (born Oppenheimer) had followed his father into the family firm to design mosaics for churches. Not until he was nearly thirty did he develop his art critical writing. Newton became much sought after as a newspaper journalist in Britain, and he frequently wrote for the *New York Times* Sunday art section. In the lecture hall and on radio his communications were clear, un-pompous and effective. And his was an approach to the Northampton *Madonna* somewhat different from Bell's: Newton wrote 'She is not part of an art-revival but a stage in art-evolution. Therefore a century hence (in 2044) she will have lost none of her potency. She will be seen as an example not of Henry Moore's sculpture but of a deep seriousness somehow inherent in the mid-twentieth century'. Again he wrote (at a later date) about this commission: 'To impose a limitation, to ask an artist to conform to the rules of a game that is unfamiliar to him, may be a positive source of inspiration'.[21]

Ten years younger than Newton was Hussey's third champion, Kenneth Clark. Son of a wealthy thread manufacturer, Clark enjoyed the fullest possible career in art. He was formed most critically by the two years he spent at Villa I Tatti near Florence, working with Bernard Berenson. Appointed director of the National Gallery in London and also surveyor of the King's Pictures at the age of 30, he was for five decades never far from the centre of the high art scene in Britain. Respected, invited and honoured widely in Europe, in America and in Australia, he moved in intellectual circles with a patrician authority and exquisite manners. Only in his case would it not be seen as folly, pride or condescension to make a pioneering public television series entitled *Civilization* (1969). While Clark's commendation of the Moore sculpture itself was wholehearted — he commended the church for employing 'a sculptor who worked in a living style' when he addressed the congregation at the unveiling of the statue — in his correspondence we nevertheless find a hint of pessimism about the very possibility of a Christian Art. He took the position that so overwhelming was the tradition of art imagery within the Christian history that today's artists might properly only copy or paraphrase old masters. 'It is almost impossible for living artists to invent, with any conviction, scenes which have been given such perfect expression by the great artists of the past'. He continues, not without a hint of the patronising, 'but it is an interesting task for any painter to translate these images into the colour and handling of modern painting'. About Moore, however, Clark wrote this to Hussey:

> I need hardly tell you how much in sympathy I am with your idea that Henry Moore should do a Madonna and Child for your church. I consider him the greatest living sculptor and it is of the utmost importance that the Church should employ artists of first-rate talent instead of the mediocrities usually employed. As you will have seen from the models which he showed you yesterday, he has thought out the problem of the Madonna and Child most seriously and his sketches promise that this will be one of his finest works. I am sure that it will shed great

lustre on your church, and congratulate you on it most warmly.[22]

With three such individual champions as Bell, Newton and Clark, the Moore statue was launched on its ministry in the Church of England and beyond. Opposition, shrill at first, faltered soon and then failed.

Moore was to complete three more works for Anglican churches. A circular altar (Plate 2 and Front Cover) carved in Travertine was finished in 1972, having been commissioned for St. Stephen's, Walbrook, by Peter Palumbo, one of the church-wardens of the parish. Installed in 1985, in this Wren's most important parish church in the City of London, following an exemplarily thorough and careful restoration, it has been the focus of much legal, liturgical and aesthetic discussion.

Another *Madonna and Child* (1948, Hornton stone, 48 inches high), commissioned as a war memorial in 1948 for St. Peter's, Claydon, in Suffolk, can now be seen in nearby St. Mary the Virgin, Barham, where it was removed in 1978 when the first church was declared redundant. This image (Plate 3) was developed from the largest of the maquettes Moore prepared for Northampton.

The last of Moore's works discussed here, *Mother and Child: Hood* (1983, Travertine marble, 72 inches high), has since 1984 been on loan from the Henry Moore Foundation to St. Paul's Cathedral, London (plate 4). An American con-nexion can be detected in its form, a form of protectiveness and vulnerability. The connexion is with the early *Two Forms* (1934, Pynkado wood, base length 21 inches), which was the first Moore to be bought outside Britain by the Museum of Modern Art in New York City and by Alfred Barr, its first director. Here (plate 5) for the first time Moore divided his shapes, and the art lies in the relating of the one to the other. This dividing theme recurs in Moore's work since the 1930s and is given a theological context in this last *Mother and Child*. Here the tension in the relation of every child with its mother is explored in respect of Jesus and Mary. The child is here related (attached?) ambiguously: the two figures have at least their Travertine veins in common, but the child is held vulnerably, dangerously: it might drop and fall. This child is not bound to its parent by each and every aspect of the familiar ties which in fact or in regret bind every man to his mother. Here Moore's two forms address not the gospel narrative, but the sheer mystery of the Word made flesh.[23]

Hussey's eye, and his prayer in the first place, sparked into being the Church of England's greatest twentieth century sculptures. He caused Moore's great powers to be brought to bear on the mystery which both theology and art need one another to present and to celebrate. Like John Keble, Hussey developed friendships with artists. The two men, each in their day, approached their commissioning work in a serious spirit, respecting the demands of the church of their time. In so doing, they provide a paradigm for any who would be gratefully remembered for their alterations to the fabric entrusted to their care.

Notes

1. T. Mozley, *Reminiscences, Chiefly of Oriel College and the Oxford Movement*, 2nd ed. (London: Longmans, Green & Co., 1882), 1:217.
2. See James F. White, *The Cambridge Movement, The Ecclesiologists and the Gothic Revival* (Cambridge: University Press, 1962).
3. Eleanor A. Towle, *John Mason Neale: A Memoir*, 2nd ed. (London: Longmans, Green & Co., 1907), 68, 76.
4. Paul Thompson, *William Butterfield* (London: Routledge and K. Paul, 1971).
5. See Sister Charles Murray, 'Artistic Idiom and Doctrinal Development,' in *The Making of Orthodoxy: Essays in Honour of Henry Chadwick*, ed. Rowan Williams (Cambridge: University Press, 1989), 288–307.
6. See H.E. Symonds, *The Council of Trent and Anglican Formularies*, (Oxford: H. Milford, 1933); esp., chapter XV 'Images'.
7. Sir Robert Phillimore, *The Principal Ecclesiastical Judgments, delivered in the Court of Arches 1867–1875*, (London: Rivingtons, 1876), 380–82.
8. G.W.O. Addleshaw and F. Etchells, *The Architectural Setting of Anglican Worship* (London: Faber and Faber, 1948), 161–62; see also Nigel Yates, *Buildings, Faith and Worship: The Liturgical Arrangement of Anglican Churches 1600–1900* (Oxford: University Press, 1991).
9. G.H. and G.L. Newsom, *The Faculty Jurisdiction of the Church of England*, 2nd ed. (London: Sweet and Maxwell, 1993).

10. Shakespeare, *Sonnet 66*.
11. 'Inventory of the Pictures belonging to the Earl of Leicester, 1588', Notes and Queries, 3rd ser., ii, 201, 224.
12. John Dillenberger, *Benjamin West: The Context of His Life's Work* (San Antonio: Trinity University Press, 1977).
13. See John Dillenberger, *The Visual Arts and Christianity in America; the Colonial Period through the Nineteenth Century*, rev.ed. (New York: Crossroads, 1988); also, Jane Dillenberger and Joshua C. Taylor, *The Hand and the Spirit: Religious Art in America 1700–1900* (Berkeley: University Art Museum, 1972).
14. See Walter Hussey, *Patron of Art: The Revival of a Great Tradition among Modern Artists* (London: Weidenfeld and Nicolson, 1985); The *Times* obituary of Hussey appeared on July 26, 1985.
15. See Roger Berthoud, *The Life of Henry Moore* (New York: E.P. Dutton, 1987).
16. Edgar Wind, *The Eloquence of Symbols: Studies in Humanist Art*, ed. Jaynie Anderson (Oxford: Clarendon Press, 1983); esp. chapter XI 'Traditional Religion and Modern Art'.
17. Letter of Henry Moore to Walter Hussey, August 26, 1943, quoted in Hussey, op.cit., 33.
18. See R.C.D. Jasper, *George Bell Bishop of Chichester*, (London: Oxford University Press, 1967); esp. chapter 7, 'The Church and the Arts,' 121–34.
19. Bell, 'The Church and the Artist,' in *The Studio*, 124 (September 1942): 91–92.
20. *The Listener*, January 13, 1955.
21. Eric Newton, 'Henry Moore's *Madonna and Child*,' in *The Architectural Review*, 95 (May 1944): 190.
22. Letter of Kenneth Clark to Walter Hussey, July 26, 1943, quoted in Hussey, op.cit., 30.
23. See my 'Moore's Church Sculptures,' in *Church Building* (Winter 1986): 4.